Use of English

Grammar practice activities for intermediate and upper-intermediate students

Teacher's Book

Leo Jones

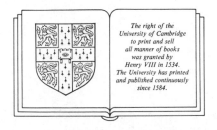

The right of the
University of Cambridge
to print and sell
all manner of books
was granted by
Henry VIII in 1534.
The University has printed
and published continuously
since 1584.

Cambridge University Press
Cambridge
London   New York   New Rochelle
Melbourne   Sydney

Published by the Press Syndicate of the University of Cambridge
The Pitt Building, Trumpington Street, Cambridge CB2 1RP
32 East 57th Street, New York, NY 10022, USA
10 Stamford Road, Oakleigh, Melbourne 3166, Australia

© Cambridge University Press 1985

First published 1985

Printed in Great Britain
at the University Press, Cambridge

ISBN 0 521 26977 6 Teacher's Book
ISBN 0 521 26976 8 Student's Book

WD

Contents

Contents

Thanks

I'm very grateful to Sue Gosling, Christine Cairns and Alison Silver for their expert advice, friendly encouragement and sharp eyes. Many thanks also to the teachers at the following schools and institutes, who used the pilot edition and made many helpful suggestions: the Bell College in Saffron Walden, the British Institute in Florence, the British School in Florence, Klubschule Migros in Basle, the Newnham Language Centre in Cambridge and the Sociedade Brasiliera de Cultura Inglesa in Sao Paulo.

LJ

The author and publishers are grateful to the authors, publishers and others who have given permission for the use of copyright material identified in the text.

Longman for the extract from the *Longman Dictionary of Contemporary English* on p. 161.
Drawings by Chris Evans.

Introduction

Aims

Use of English is a book of revision activities for intermediate to upper-intermediate students who:
− still make many grammatical errors
− lack confidence in using English in conversation and in writing
− feel safer using the simplest grammatical structures
− find it difficult to use a variety of structures
− need to improve their spoken and written English for a forthcoming examination.

By using the activities and exercises in this book, students will:
− improve their accuracy in speech and in writing
− develop a feeling for accuracy
− learn to correct their own errors
− use English more creatively in communicative activities and tasks
− extend their range of expression.

The book covers all the main 'problem areas' of English grammar and usage that are required knowledge for the Cambridge First Certificate exam. The syllabus is based on a detailed analysis of Cambridge examination papers and on the writer's own experience of teaching intermediate and upper-intermediate learners from many different countries.

Description of the material

Each unit in *Use of English* contains a variety of activities, some of which are fairly closely controlled, others more open-ended. Some of the activities may be done orally, others should be done in writing, sometimes after a brief discussion. Several different aspects of a grammatical area and different uses of the same forms may be covered in one unit and, for this reason, the activities do not all lead 'logically' on from each other. The contrast between different kinds of activity within the same unit will help to 'refresh' students' motivation throughout the lesson.

The material in *Use of English* is not intended to be students' first contact with the grammatical points covered. Most of the grammar involved will already have 'come up' in previous, more elementary courses and been experienced in reading or listening material. There is, therefore, no explicit input phase in each unit. The first activity in each unit generally sets the

1

scene for the activities that follow by means of a short dialogue, some illustrated examples or an introductory practice exercise. Any explanation of grammatical points should arise from the questions that students ask and from the errors that they make.

Of course, within the book there are sure to be several points that students do not immediately recognise or understand. These must be dealt with as and when the need arises. In other words, this is not a comprehensive grammar book that sets out to explain and practise the whole of English grammar. Rather, it is a revision course where using English in practice activities allows students first to discover which areas of English they are stronger or weaker in and then to set about improving their weaknesses. Students must be encouraged to participate in this process, to ask questions if they are puzzled, and not to sit back and expect to be 'taught' to use English accurately.

Using this book

Use of English is designed to be used as the 'accuracy' component of a balanced course for intermediate and upper-intermediate students. It can, for example, be used in parallel with material which emphasises oral fluency and listening skills, such as *Ideas**. Alternatively, it can be used as part of a course for students who need to improve their spoken and written accuracy and who may be taking the Cambridge First Certificate or a similar exam and who are using an exam preparation book, such as *Progress towards First Certificate**. It might also be used as a preliminary course in grammatical accuracy for students who will later be using more advanced material where a good knowledge of English grammar is presupposed, such as *Functions of English**. In short, any students who need to improve their grammatical accuracy will find the material in this book both useful and enjoyable.

No class is likely to work systematically through *Use of English* unit by unit from beginning to end, even though the earlier units are rather easier than the later ones. The teacher using this material will need to decide where his or her particular class's weaknesses lie and to concentrate on the units which cover those areas. Although a more advanced class may benefit from dipping into the material here and there, the average intermediate and upper-intermediate class will find that most of the material is useful, though probably not every activity will need to be studied for an equal length of time. The order of the units in the book can be changed according to the needs of a particular class, but it is not recommended that units which are grouped together are taken out of sequence. (For example, unit 15 should not be done before units 13 and 14.)

Of course, as a revision course, *Use of English* can't cover everything. The teacher has an essential role to play in correcting errors or, preferably, encouraging self-correction. Everyone learning a language makes errors and

*By Leo Jones, published by Cambridge University Press.

it takes time for these to be eliminated, even when they are the kind of 'silly mistakes' which the student knows to be wrong. Many difficulties are unforeseeable: they may be personal to an individual student or they may be particular to the nationality you teach. Only the class teacher is qualified to deal with such difficulties and this book sets out to provide plenty of practice material for the teacher to use. However, it cannot anticipate all the errors everyone is going to make. The material depends on the skill and experience of the teacher and on the active participation of the students themselves to succeed fully.

The teacher and the class

Most of the activities in *Use of English* are designed to be done by students working together in small groups or in pairs. In some cases, particularly in small classes and where the teacher wants to keep a check on accuracy, activities can be done as a whole class, treated as one large group. Even in these cases, however, students should be urged to explore and experiment with English, and not just work through the exercises mechanically as if they were drills. Teachers who feel that their classes need to spend time on pattern drills at this level will have to devise their own supplementary material. This is not the kind of Teacher's Book which provides a plethora of mechanical drills, because such drills are of little benefit to students at this level. Only by using English creatively can students develop their ability to actually use English to express their own ideas. Students who can only do exercises, answer quickly in drills and write sentences are not going to be successful in using English as a means of communication.

Students should not be corrected all the time and made to feel vulnerable when they speak. The atmosphere in class should be relaxed and co-operative, not tense and competitive. In this way, students are more likely to enjoy their lessons, acquire more English and make progress. If they feel worried or defensive, then they are not likely to enjoy their lessons nor make any progress – they may even stop coming to class.

The advantages of students working together in pairs or small groups far outweigh the disadvantages: everyone gets a chance to speak and to experiment with their English and they feel much less inhibited when they are not expected to perform in front of the rest of the class. (Shy or quiet students often become quite talkative when in small groups.) The main disadvantage is that errors may go uncorrected, but provided that the teacher is alert and students themselves are aware of the '**relevant errors**' (see below), then many errors will be spotted and students will correct themselves or each other. The teacher's role during these group activities is to move from group to group eavesdropping, showing an interest, offering suggestions or advice, keeping track of the progress of the activity and deciding when to call a halt, making notes of errors to be discussed afterwards, and by his or her very presence or ubiquity discouraging students from using their native language.

Even the activities indicated by ![symbol], where students are expected to write their answers, can be done by students working together. The discussion involved in producing a collaborative set of answers is both enjoyable and beneficial and it is recommended that this approach is used wherever possible. Sometimes, however, to provide variety or a change of pace, students may be asked to do such exercises on their own.

There are advantages and disadvantages in students having a 'regular partner' in class. On the one hand, a regular pair can become an efficient working team who enjoy each other's company and stimulate each other; on the other hand regular partners may become stale or tired of each other and if they are not well-matched they may hold each other up. It makes sense therefore to ring the changes and to give everyone a chance to be everyone else's partner at some stage in their course.

Writing

In each unit there is at least one exercise, indicated by the symbol ![symbol], which should be done in writing. In some units there are several of these. Writing is an extremely valuable way of developing accuracy and, as suggested above, it need not be a solitary activity or even a boring one if such exercises are done collaboratively by students working together.

Besides the exercises shown with the ![symbol] symbol, there are short written phases in many of the other activities in *Use of English*. These usually involve nothing more time-consuming than writing a few sentences or making notes. Some students find that writing helps them to focus their attention and remember better, and if your students find writing helpful in this way you should introduce a short written phase whenever possible into otherwise oral activities. To leave the teacher free to decide when to do this, only those

exercises which *must* be done in writing have the ![symbol] symbol in the Student's Book.

The last exercise in each unit can be set as homework. The value of written homework as a consolidation of what has been practised in class cannot be overemphasised. Students unwilling to do such homework may need to be persuaded that doing it will help them to remember what they have done in class. They can perhaps be reassured that none of the final exercises in *Use of English* are very long! However, if preferred, any of the final exercises can be done in class.

Acquisition and learning

Some recent research into the way in which adults learn a foreign language suggests that there is a difference between 'acquiring' a second language and 'learning' it. Stephen Krashen's work, described in *Second Language*

Acquisition and Second Language Learning (Pergamon 1981) and in his other books, is of particular interest and he has developed the 'Monitor Theory'. Briefly, according to this theory, language 'acquisition' is a subconscious process which results in a working knowledge of the language and how it is used, whereas 'learning' is a conscious process which may only lead to knowledge *about* it. In fluent speech the successful student will use his or her 'acquired' knowledge without thinking, and accuracy (successful mastery of the rules of grammar in use) will develop gradually, as 'acquisition' occurs at its natural speed through exposure to more and more grammar in communicative contexts. However, most students will need to refer to their 'learned' knowledge when deciding whether something is correct or incorrect – particularly in writing, which (unlike speech) can be performed at one's own speed and where inaccuracy is likely to be more noticeable. This ability to 'monitor' one's own accuracy, especially in writing, is a skill that students do need to have but it is likely to be a hindrance if it is over-used and hampers fluent communication. A student who is preoccupied with accuracy is unlikely to be able to use English very well in conversation.

The material in *Use of English*, focussing as it does on accuracy, may be seen at first glance as rather retrogressive by teachers who (like me) are attracted towards the 'Monitor Theory'. However, by the time most students reach the intermediate or upper-intermediate level they need to 'polish' or 'fine tune' their English, to eliminate persistent errors and to become more accurate, particularly in writing. Moreover, as most examinations demand accurate English, inaccuracy is a handicap which loses marks. Indeed many exam questions in, for example, the Cambridge First Certificate Use of English paper, unfortunately seem designed to trap candidates into making errors. Students who hope to succeed in such exams need to be capable of 'monitoring' their own English and the material in this book will help them to develop this skill in an enjoyable way. But also in this book there are activities where they can concentrate on using English for communication. (*Ideas** contains an abundance of communicative activities for students who need to develop their fluency further.)

Accuracy and fluency

With the development of communicative language teaching, the importance of accuracy has sometimes been neglected in favour of encouraging fluency in spoken English. It seems clear that a balanced approach where both fluency and accuracy are developed is essential if students are to do more than simply 'survive' in English-speaking situations.

A student who, for example, is only going to use English in informal conversations with good friends (who will be prepared to make allowances for grammatical errors) may not need to improve his or her accuracy.

*By Leo Jones, published by Cambridge University Press.

Students who may need to participate in conversations with strangers or with foreign colleagues or acquaintances cannot 'get by' all the time by speaking fluent inaccurate English, though people are normally prepared to tolerate a foreign accent and occasional errors. A very inaccurate speaker may even find that people are listening to his or her mistakes, not to what he or she is trying to say!

In writing, inaccuracy is an even greater handicap since errors are far more noticeable to a reader than spoken errors are to a listener. This applies to formal or informal letters but, for many students, it is examinations which are the ultimate test of accuracy in writing. A student who can't write without making lots of errors is likely to fail most English exams.

This book provides practice material for students who need to improve their accuracy in speech and in writing. There are also activities which are designed to develop both accuracy *and* fluency and give students a chance to communicate in English.

Correction

Students cannot suddenly and miraculously achieve accuracy in spoken English. The best that can be hoped for is a progressive improvement in accuracy. Correction is an essential tool to guide students towards improvement but there is no point in correcting every error that is made. Instead, the teacher should concentrate on correcting **relevant errors**. Relevant errors are errors concerned with the theme of the unit: verb forms in unit 3 and prepositions in unit 8, but not vice versa.

Even though most of the activities in this book focus on accuracy, the teacher must be extremely gentle and tactful when correcting errors. Sensitive or diffident students often feel that they are being reprimanded or even mocked if they are told they are 'wrong'. Even well-adjusted average students can be upset by tactless or aggressive correction techniques.

It is recommended that correction is seen by the teacher and students as a *positive* act, designed to help students to improve their accuracy, and never as an implied criticism. In fact, rather than announcing a correction to a student or even saying 'No, that's not quite right', the teacher should encourage self-correction. This can be done gently and tactfully as the following examples show:

Student: What you did yesterday?
Teacher: Pardon?
Student: I mean, what did you do yesterday?

Student: I'm interesting in painting.
Teacher: Um?
Student: Sorry, I'm interested in painting.

Student: I enjoy to watch TV.
(Teacher raises eyebrows or lifts forefinger slightly to indicate error.)
Student: Er . . . I enjoy watching TV.

Student: I'm interested for football.
Teacher: Interested for?
Student: No, I mean, interested *in* football.

If such techniques fail, the conversation can continue and the other members of the group (or class) can be asked to suggest a correction, like this:

Student: I've seen her yesterday.
Teacher: I'm sorry?
Student: I said: I've seen her yesterday.
Teacher: Well, that's not *quite* right. Can anyone help?

Provided that this kind of peer correction is offered in a spirit of helpfulness and camaraderie, with no hint of derision or superiority, it can be a useful correction technique.

Sometimes, however, time can be saved by the teacher offering a correction after the student has had a chance to correct him or herself. Again, this should be done kindly and tactfully by saying, for example: 'I think you mean you *saw* her yesterday' or 'It's probably better to say "If I *were* you".'

In case you feel the advice given above seems too tender-hearted, let me reassure you that it may be wise to treat over-confident students less compassionately and, sometimes at least, to actually say 'No, that's wrong'! The important thing to get across to students is that it is not the person that's wrong, but their English that's wrong.

During group activities and pair work the teacher should be constantly flitting from group to group, sometimes interrupting in the ways suggested above. Often, however, such interruptions may be unwelcome or intrusive, and correction should occur after the activity has finished. The teacher can make notes of the *relevant* errors he or she overhears and later ask the class to make comments. The students who made the errors need not be identified if the teacher begins: 'I heard someone say . . . ' or 'One of you said . . . ' or 'What's wrong with this sentence? . . . ' This kind of feedback session is essential after each activity but the teacher should be careful to encourage and praise the class as well as criticising them. It's more motivating to say 'That was really very good! Well done!' than 'Right, now here are all the mistakes you made . . . ' This feedback session also gives students a chance to ask any questions about the language they require to perform the activity better and, as already emphasised, such questions should be encouraged.

Written work should be treated in a similar way: the teacher should under-line the relevant errors and get the students to make their own corrections. If a student cannot improve parts of his or her own work, then a partner should be asked to help before the teacher is consulted. As with spoken English, the teacher should concentrate on the relevant errors, encouraging self-correction of these. Other errors should be simply corrected by writing the correct form above. The example below is part of a paragraph written in unit 3. The relevant errors in this unit are those connected with verb forms. (Written work of this type should be done on alternate lines to allow space for self-correction later.)

John and Mary <u>was</u> married and for the first few years they were very happy. As time*s* go on they <u>start</u> to get bored with ~~they~~ ^{each} other and

The Teacher's Book

The notes for each activity suggest ways of handling the material and give helpful hints and extra ideas. There is also a key to the exercises, where necessary. In some activities, there are extra language items that can be introduced for students who are finding things rather too undemanding and who might get bored while the others are still benefiting from the activity.

At the beginning of each unit in the Teacher's Book there is a **Summary** of the grammatical and other points covered in the unit. This Summary gives the teacher an overview of the grammar involved, but it is not intended to be a full description of the rules such as a grammar reference book would provide. Teachers who need the reassurance of a more complete description of grammar and usage should refer to *Practical English Usage* by Michael Swan (Oxford University Press 1980). In each Summary the relevant sections in this book are indicated.

After the Summary in the Teacher's Book there is a list of **Relevant errors**. These are examples of the typical kind of errors which may occur during the activities and exercises in the unit. These are the kind of errors which should be corrected immediately or which students should be asked to correct themselves – see the section on Correction above.

Within each unit there is at least one **Extra activity**, suggested at the relevant points between the activities in the Student's Book. These can be introduced to add variety or a change of pace to the lesson – or used as surprises that only you, the teacher, know about. Again, it's up to you to decide which of these activities to use. They are placed in the Teacher's Book because they work best when introduced personally by the teacher, not because they are less important than the material in the Student's Book.

At the very end of the Teacher's Book is a 'route map' of the **Communication activities**, indicated by the symbol ▓. The directions that should be given to students for these activities are given in both the Student's Book and the Teacher's Book in the relevant place in the unit itself. In these activities there is an 'information gap' between the participants (working in pairs or sometimes larger groups), who have to communicate to bridge the gap and share or exchange information. Some of the longer exercises have a key concealed somewhere among the communication activities – only the Teacher's Book reveals which these are and where they are to be found, to prevent students from 'cheating'.

The less confident or less experienced teacher should read carefully through unit 1 in the Teacher's Book. These notes are more detailed than the notes for later units and contain an explanation of some of the principles underlying the activities in the book. After doing the first unit with a class, a quick re-read of the Introduction to the Teacher's Book is recommended to help you to feel totally at home with the techniques used in *Use of English*.

1 QUESTIONS: *Wh-* and *Yes/No* questions

Summary

The various activities in this unit cover the areas shown below. For a detailed explanation of the rules involved, the teacher should consult a reference book such as *Practical English Usage*, as indicated below.

Practice in forming and using *yes/no* and *Wh-* questions with the appropriate intonation:

What did you do yesterday?   *Is this correct?*
Who gave you the book?   *Did you see John last night?*

Using a full range of question words:

who, where, when, why, what, what else, what ... for, which, how, how many, how much, how long

Using indirect question forms in polite questions:

Could you tell me where the museum is?
I'd like to know if you've been to London.
Would you mind telling me what you saw there?

For a full description of the rules of usage involved, refer to *Practical English Usage* by Michael Swan (Oxford University Press 1980) sections 511, 512, 513 and 535.

Relevant errors

The errors listed here are the kind of errors that should be corrected if they are made during the activities in this unit. Wherever possible, encourage students to correct themselves, if they can, before you offer your own corrections. It is unlikely that any class will make all of these errors, but you may well recognise among them several that members of your own particular class make.

☆ What you did yesterday?   ☆ Who did the cake eat?
☆ What means 'space invader'?   ☆ What drank she?
☆ What does mean 'alien'?   ☆ Who to did you give the book?
☆ What you are doing here?   ☆ Who you gave the book?
☆ I'd like to know when are you leaving.
☆ Could you tell me do you understand?

(The symbol ☆ denotes an incorrect sentence.)

Space invader

AS A CLASS AND IN PAIRS

1 Ask the class to suggest some of the questions that the journalists might be asking the space invader in the cartoon. First of all, students might work this out together in pairs before suggestions are made by the whole class. Some possible questions might be:

Who have you come to see?
Where have you come from?
What has impressed you so far about this planet?
When are you planning to leave here?
How did you travel from your world to ours?
Why did you come here?
What else has impressed you about the Earth?

2 Before asking students to work out questions for the three interviews, it might be enjoyable and worthwhile to get the class to hold a press conference and to interview *you* in the role of the President of the USA, or a member of the British Royal Family (Princess Diana, for example), or a favourite film star, or someone who has been in the news recently.

Make sure that each pair writes down at least five questions for each interview so that, when the list is passed on to a neighbouring pair, the next pair has 15 or more questions to answer.

3 As a reminder of the kind of questions that can be asked and also to ensure that a variety of question forms are used, write on the board the following ways of starting questions:

Who	How	Which
Where	How long	When
What	How much	Why
What else	How many	

Students who find the material in this and in later activities unchallenging may find it useful to be reminded of some ways in which we can delay answering questions or gain 'thinking time' before answering:

Well, . . .
Let me see, . . .
That's a good question . . .
I'm not really sure.
I couldn't tell you off hand.
I don't really know.
I'm afraid I can't answer that one.

11

➤→ **Extra activity**

AS A CLASS

The following activity can be introduced to add variety to the lesson, or a change of pace. It will also be a surprise element because it is not in the Student's Book and will appear to come from you, the teacher, rather than from the book itself.

Draw the incomplete sketch on the left on the board and tell the class you're going to tell them how to complete it. But they must ask you questions to find out the missing details. Answer each question briefly but clearly and make sure everyone draws each detail you give in their notebooks. Encourage the quieter ones to ask questions as well as the more confident ones.

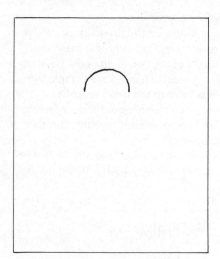 

It's not very clear

IN PAIRS

Each member of the pair is given different information (one of the photos reproduced sharply and with more detail) and the task consists of bridging the 'information gap'.
Student A looks at activity 1 (on page 99 at the back of the book)
Student B looks at activity 6 (on page 101 at the back of the book)
A third student should share A or B's activity.

While the pairs are doing this activity, go round the class eavesdropping. Make sure everyone is doing what they are supposed to be doing and not 'cheating' by looking at each other's photos. Only at the end of the activity is anyone allowed to peek, when you give permission. As you eavesdrop, listen carefully for relevant errors (see above) and ask students to correct them-selves if this can be done without interrupting the conversations unhelpfully. Make a note of the important points you want to draw everyone's attention to.

After the activity has been stopped and peeking has been allowed, ask the class if there are any questions they wish to ask about the activity and the language items they needed to use. Praise the points you thought were praiseworthy as well as asking the class to correct the errors you overheard and have noted down.

➥ **Extra activity**

IN PAIRS

This is a similar activity to the one above, for students who need further practice with another information gap exercise.

Using picture cards made of photos from magazines stuck onto stiff card, students in pairs can ask each other questions to find out as much as they can about their partner's photograph. The photos should not be shown until the questioner has a clear idea of what is shown.

It may be helpful here to introduce the different intonations that can be used when saying *Yes* or *No* and the different meanings conveyed. This will need to be demonstrated as well as written on the board. You could do this by yourself pretending to be a very famous person and getting the class to find out who you are by asking questions that you can only answer with *Yes* or *No*, but with different intonations:

Yes ↓	*No* ↓	abrupt, certain, self-assured
Yyes ⌄	*Nnno* ⌄	less certain, more ambiguous answer
Yeees ⌃	*Nooo* ⌃	encouraging, humorous

If you feel this may be too difficult for your class, get them to plunge straight into the activity. Go round monitoring each pair and listen out for any relevant errors.

Yes or No?

IN PAIRS

Perhaps first show everyone what to do by getting the whole class to ask questions about one or two people *you* have in mind (King Henry VIII? Queen Elizabeth I? William Shakespeare?). Demonstrate the use of *Yes, in a way* and *Not exactly* as you answer, as well as the different possible intonations of *Yes* and *No* shown above. When everyone knows what to do, allow a little time for each student to write down secretly the names of three or four famous people that their partner must ask questions about. Go round the class listening in to as many different pairs as you can. Afterwards, perhaps get one student to challenge the whole class to find out one of his or her people by asking questions all together.

➤→ **Extra activity**

AS A CLASS

Further practice in asking *Yes* or *No* questions can be supplied by playing the well-known 'Yes/No Game'. The idea of the game is to trap each 'contestant' into saying *Yes* or *No* in answer to the class's questions. Clever 'contestants' can go on avoiding *Yes* or *No* by saying things like 'That's true' or 'It isn't' for quite some time.

A whistle or bell is needed to give the game the right kind of showbiz atmosphere!

I'd like to know . . .

AS A CLASS AND IN PAIRS

The aim of this activity is to show the need for politeness when asking personal questions or when talking to people in more formal language. The indirect question forms may cause further relevant errors, particularly in word order. Students are likely to find this activity more difficult than some of the previous activities.

1 After getting the class to explain the need for appropriacy, allow time for everyone to write down five similar questions and go round helping or offering suggestions while they're doing this. Take a sample of some of the sentences written down – there won't be time to hear them all, and in any case this would probably be awfully repetitive.

2 It may be necessary to allow the 'reporters' a little time to prepare their lines of questioning (but not to write down the exact words of every question). The 'reporters' could all be put in a group together to do this preparation while the 'famous people' decide who they're going to be and whether they know enough about 'themselves' to answer any foreseeable questions.

Listen carefully to the pairs at work and make a note of any errors that you should comment on later. Allow time for questions about the language items afterwards.

Where were you on the night of 13 May?

This exercise should be done in writing. If it is done in class, students could decide together in pairs or small groups on a collaborative version, which is then written down and handed in for your comments. Alternatively, you may prefer to have students working on the exercise on their own and then comparing versions with each other before handing their work in. Or, if there is little time left, the work can be given as homework.

In correcting the written work, try to distinguish between relevant errors and other errors. Write in corrections only of the other errors and get students to work out for themselves how the underlined relevant errors should be corrected. (See **Correction** in the Introduction.)

In the suggested model version below there are a number of suitable variations possible.

Detective: Where *were you on the night of 13 May?*

Suspect: At the cinema.

Detective: What *was the name of the film you saw?*

Suspect: I don't remember the name, I'm afraid.

Detective: When *did you come out of the cinema?*

Suspect: Oh, about 11 o'clock, I suppose.

Detective: Who *did you go to the cinema with?*

Suspect: No one, I went alone.

Detective: Where *did you go after you left the cinema?*

Suspect: I went straight home then.

Detective: What *time did you arrive home?*

Suspect: At midnight.

2 QUESTIONS: *Isn't it* questions

Summary

Practice in forming and using negative questions and question-tags:
Isn't that your ex-wife?
Didn't she once live in Austria?

She's living in Switzerland now, isn't she?
She isn't living in England any more, is she?
That's her husband, isn't it?
There's a lot of difference between them, isn't there?
She left you ten years ago, didn't she?
I'm being very nosy, aren't I?
I'm not being too curious, am I?
This interview won't take long, will it?

Using appropriate intonation in negative questions and question-tags:
Isn't it Monday today? ⤴ – rising intonation indicates that the speaker is fairly certain but is **making sure** he or she is right.
It's Monday today, isn't it? ⤴ – rising intonation indicates that the speaker is unsure and is **finding out** if he or she is right.
It's Monday today, isn't it? ⤵ – falling intonation indicates that the speaker is certain but is **getting agreement** from the listener, perhaps as a way of keeping the conversation going.

(For a full description of the rules of usage involved, refer to *Practical English Usage* sections 511, 514 and 515.)

Relevant errors

☆ You aren't from here, isn't it?
☆ You don't like it, don't you?
☆ I'm right this time, amn't I?
☆ He can't understand, is he?
☆ It's Monday today, isn't it? (with inappropriate intonation)

☆ It isn't very good, isn't it?
☆ Isn't this not fun?
☆ Is not this fun?
☆ He'd done it, isn't he?

Making sure

AS A CLASS

Make sure that students use the appropriate intonation for questions of this type. Allow time for them to write down the missing verb forms – this can be done collaboratively in pairs.

Didn't we meet at Bruce's party?
Wasn't it Bruce who introduced us?
Aren't you the one who plays the piano?
Haven't you changed your hairstyle?
Didn't you use to have long hair?
Weren't you wearing a blue pullover?
Wasn't your car damaged or something?
Didn't you have to leave suddenly?

Note the distinction made in this unit between:
   'Making sure': *Isn't it Monday today?*
   'Finding out': *It's Monday, today, isn't it?* ⤴ (rising intonation)
   'Getting agreement': *It's Monday today, isn't it?* ⤵ (falling intonation)

This unit doesn't cover the kind of 'threatening' or 'sarcastic' question-tags that students should certainly be able to recognise, but which might be dangerous for them as foreigners to use themselves:
   You were ill, were you?
   So it's too hard for you, is it?
   Oh, you don't like my attitude, don't you?

Didn't you go to the cinema?

IN PAIRS OR GROUPS OF 3

1 To simulate an authentic 'making sure' situation, make sure that the students, working in pairs or groups of three, rely on their memories. To control the questioning and ensure that at least seven pieces of information are given, write up this table on the board:

Last week: M   Tu   W   Th   F   Sa   Su

2 Only when they have been separated should the members of the pairs or groups be allowed to make notes. These notes must be scribbled down quickly, using just one word or phrase for each item to be remembered.
3 Then, when each couple or group is reunited, the conversations can start. Monitor the activity and listen out for relevant errors.

17

Finding out

IN PAIRS OR GROUPS OF 3 OR 4

This exercise explores the grammatical problems involved in question-tags. It is best done collaboratively in pairs or small groups. The trickiest ones are likely to be . . . *aren't I?* and . . . *isn't there?*

Find out whether the students can use the appropriate intonation and, if necessary, do some quick repetition practice.

You didn't come here by bus, *did you?*

You came in a flying saucer, *didn't you?*

You come from outer space, *don't you?*

That isn't very near here, *is it?*

It was a long, tiring journey, *wasn't it?*

We look different from each other, *don't we?*

You've got three eyes, *haven't you?*

You're not wearing a hat, *are you?*

There's no hair on your head, *is there?*

You can understand what I say, *can't you?*

I'm speaking slowly enough for you, *aren't I?*

You'll come and have some tea with me, *won't you?*

▶→ Extra activity

AS A CLASS

For further practice in manipulating 'finding out' question-tags, the following drill may be useful. However, don't rush through it expecting everyone to produce perfect responses – instead, stop when necessary to discuss the problems and ask for alternative responses.

Ask students to reply as politely as possible, even though your statements are going to sound somewhat silly. Appropriate responses will involve question-tags with rising intonation. Begin by saying:

'I'm going to make a series of statements that you'll probably disagree with. Please answer politely. Here are a couple of examples to show you what you've got to do . . . '

Teacher says:	*Student replies:*
I think 2 + 2 is 3.	No, it's 4, isn't it? ⤴ *(rising intonation)*
I suppose three 7s are 22.	No, they're 21, aren't they?
Lemons are always blue.	No, they're *yellow*, aren't they?

Napoleon was a German.	No, he was a *Frenchman*, wasn't he?
Jupiter is the nearest planet to the sun.	No, *Mercury* is the nearest, isn't it?
3 × 3 is 6.	etc.
Children are stronger than adults.	
The USA used to be a German colony.	
The Beatles were a famous football team.	
Beethoven was a great painter.	
Madrid is the capital of France.	
Cigarettes are good for your health.	
They speak Spanish in Portugal.	
Pelé used to be a great tennis star.	
Yesterday was Saturday.	
It's now 6.35.	
This lesson started three minutes ago.	
There are 49 students in this class.	
We've known each other for 13 years.	
Our next meal will be breakfast.	

Getting agreement

ALONE AND THEN IN PAIRS

1 The first part must be done by each student alone (no peeking allowed!) so that there is a reasonably genuine information gap in part 2.
2 Although this exercise is rather artificial, it will enable students to get a clear idea of whether they can control the use of question-tags easily. Listen carefully for appropriate intonation patterns.

Your favourite colour's red, isn't it?

IN GROUPS OF 3

Student A should look at communication activity 3, student B at activity 9 and student C at 12. A fourth student can share student A's information.

Taking it in turns, each student finds out some personal details from the others and tries to remember as much as possible, without making notes. Later each student attempts to recall the information, using sentences like:

'Your favourite sports are squash and badminton, aren't they?'

with the appropriate intonation (in this case either falling or rising intonation depending whether the speaker remembers clearly or is unsure). Eavesdrop on the groups and make notes for a short follow-up session afterwards.

By this time, it may be clear that some members of the class can't master question-tags however hard they try. In this case it might be reassuring to

19

point out the various ways in which one can avoid having to use question-tags:

... *I suppose.*   ... *am I right?*
... *I think.*   ... *don't you agree?*
... *as far as I know.*   ... *wouldn't you say?*

You're John Brown, aren't you?

This written exercise can be done in class, preferably collaboratively in pairs, or set as homework. The completed conversations could be 'acted out' as a final check on intonation for classes who are going to take an exam which involves reading aloud.

Several variations are possible from this suggested model version:

Interviewer: Good morning. *You're John Brown, aren't you?*

Brown: No, I'm James Brown, not John Brown.

Interviewer: I see, *and you've come about the job as salesman, haven't you?*

Brown: No, I've come about the job as a mechanic, not salesman.

Interviewer: Mechanic, eh? *Then you saw the ad in the Echo, didn't you?*

Brown: No, actually I saw the advertisement in the Times, not the Echo.

Interviewer: The Times? Well, well. *And your present employers are Anglo Engineering aren't they?*

Brown: No, my present employers are Acme Engineering.

Interviewer: Good firm! *They're the people in Tower Street, aren't they?*

Brown: No, they're the ones in Castle Lane, not Tower Street.

Interviewer: Of course. *And you've been with them for about three years, haven't you?*

Brown: Yes, I have. For just over three years now.

Interviewer: Good, good. Tell me about yourself, Mr ... er ... Mr ...

3 THE PAST: What happened?

Summary

Practice in forming and using the simple past and present perfect to ask questions and make statements about past events and experiences:

Have you ever been to South America?
When did you go to South America?
I went to Brazil in '83.
Rio was wonderful.
I've never been to Venezuela.
I didn't go to Ecuador last year.
When did you get up this morning?
Has Alan got up yet?
He got up at 7.30.
I didn't get up till noon.

Forming and using the simple past and present perfect forms of common irregular verbs and some regular verbs that can cause difficulties:

go—went—gone   *lay—laid—laid*
choose—chose—chosen   *lie—lay—lain*
leave—left—left   *lie—lied—lied*
etc.

(See *Practical English Usage* 467 and 469 for a full description.)

Relevant errors

☆ I've been there yesterday.
☆ Have you ever gone to Greece?
☆ I goed there last year.
☆ It were lovely there.
☆ What did Einstein?
☆ I've been born in 1963.
☆ He lied on the floor.
☆ He laid on the floor.
☆ He was dropping the vase on the floor.

Have you ever? 🕱

IN PAIRS

Student A should look at communication activity 5, while student B looks at
15. A third student can join forces with student A and share the information.
The idea of this activity is for students to share their experiences and find out
details of each other's activities.

Make sure everyone reads the instructions in activity 5 or 15 carefully
before they begin and, if necessary, explain the instructions in your own
words to be on the safe side. (To make things more interesting, students can
tell lies and invent experiences. Let them decide about this for themselves, as
some people may find this objectionable.)

Listen carefully as you go from pair to pair and make notes of relevant
errors that should be pointed out in the follow-up session afterwards. This
activity can be treated as a 'diagnosis' of what aspects of their use of past verb
forms the class need to improve.

It may help students with poor memories to be reminded of some ways of
referring to past time less precisely:

the other day	*a long time ago*
donkey's years ago	*ages ago*
a few weeks ago	*before you were born*
the day before yesterday	*a couple of years ago*

▶→ Extra activity

AS A CLASS

The following exercise may help students who are finding it difficult to make
the 'switch' from *have* to *did* in conversations like the ones in the activity
above. Follow this pattern in each part of the activity:

Teacher: Has anyone ever flown in a 747?
Student: Yes, I have!
Teacher: Tell us about it.
Student: Well, it was a very comfortable flight. I went from here to New
York to visit my relations there. I had a good time.
Teacher: Good, and has anyone ever flown in a DC-10?

Find out who in the class has:
  flown in a 747, or DC-10, or a helicopter, or a light plane;
  eaten oysters, or Christmas pudding, or fish and chips, or haggis;
  swum in the Atlantic, or in the Pacific, or in a lake, or in a river;
  driven a Mercedes, or a VW, or a bus, or a tractor;
  been to Scotland, or to the USA, or to France, or to Japan.

If you know your students well, you will be able to add to the ideas in the exercise to include everyone's achievements!

---

go – went – gone

IN PAIRS

1 Most students at intermediate and upper-intermediate level still have difficulty in remembering the principal parts of some irregular verbs. The incomplete table in this activity includes the 'problem verbs' as well as some that your students will find easy. Be prepared for puzzled questions when they get to the second column of verbs, but otherwise encourage each pair to solve the 'puzzles' together.

beat	beat	*beaten*	lay	*laid*	*laid*	(the table)
bite	*bit*	bitten	*lie*	lay	*lain*	(on the floor)
blow	*blew*	blown	*lie*	lied	*lied*	(= tell lies)
choose	*chose*	*chosen*	*lead*	led	*led*	
deal	dealt	*dealt*	*leave*	left	*left*	
drive	*drove*	*driven*	live	*lived*	*lived*	
eat	*ate*	*eaten*	lose	*lost*	*lost*	
fly	*flew*	flown	*rise*	rose	*risen*	
feel	*felt*	*felt*	steal	*stole*	*stolen*	
fall	fell	*fallen*	*tear*	*tore*	torn	
hide	hid	*hidden*	*throw*	*threw*	thrown	
hold	*held*	held	wear	*wore*	*worn*	

2 The sentence construction phase should be done in rather larger groups if your students are somewhat unimaginative.

You may prefer them to write 5 × 3 or even 12 × 3 sentences instead of 10 × 3 as suggested in the Student's Book.

Famous men ▣

IN PAIRS

Student A should look at activity 18, while student B looks at 26. A third student can share A's information. Make sure everyone understands what they have to do before they begin. The two lists put together give the complete, correct set of dates and names. ⟫→

Don't worry if some of the names are unfamiliar to your less knowledge-able students, and encourage them to find out from their partners who the unfamiliar men were. (Unfortunately, there don't seem to be many famous women who are well-known all over the world. However, to counteract this lack you may like to add some famous women your students will recognise.)

'My life'

IN PAIRS

1 Beginning with last year and working backwards in time, each student has to find out about *each year* of his or her partner's life. To start things off, get the class to ask you questions about recent years in your own life. Perhaps write the last 20 or so years on the board in reverse order (1984, 1983, 1982, 1982, etc.) to ensure that no years are left out in the conver-sations.
2 Rearrange the pairs so that everyone has someone different to talk to. You may only need to move one student from the far left to the far right (or from the very front to the very back) to achieve this.

➤→ Extra activity

IN GROUPS OF 4 OR 5

This game gives extra practice in asking and answering questions about past experiences and in narrating. First of all, prepare a slip of paper for each member of the class. Write LIAR on enough slips for one member of each group to get one, and write TRUTH on all the rest. Then, making sure one and only one member of each group gets a LIAR slip, distribute the slips without letting anyone peek. The idea of the game is to tell a story about one's past: a good theme is A HOLIDAY I REMEMBER. The liars' stories will be fiction and all the others will be telling the truth.

Allow a few moments for everyone to remember and prepare their stories, making notes if necessary. Then each member of the group tells his or her story and answers questions from the others. The group has to decide who is the liar among them and explain how they decided this.

A variation is to have a random number of liars in each group, but this does make it harder to play the game and may be more complicated to set up.

One fine day . . .

IN GROUPS OF 4, THEN IN PAIRS

1 Students should begin by working out their version of the story in groups of about 4.
2 Then the groups should be split up and pairs formed of members of different groups. If necessary, one 'pair' can be a trio from different groups. Each partner has to tell his or her group's story.
3 The story should probably be written as homework, since this might be too time-consuming to be done in class.
4 Before the written stories are handed in to the teacher, get students to read each other's work and comment on it. When marking the work, distinguish between relevant errors and other errors.

(The 'correct' sequence of pictures begins with the couple having a meal, then watching TV, getting a cat, sitting on the sofa with a fatter cat, playing with the kittens and finally sitting on the floor.)

4 THE PAST: What was happening?

Summary

Practice in forming and using the past progressive to ask questions and make statements about simultaneous events, actions that began before a point in time and continued after, or which were interrupted:

He was watching TV while she was doing the washing up.
What were you doing at 2.30 this morning?
She was washing up when the TV blew up.

Understanding the different meanings of the simple past, past progressive and past perfect in sentences like:

I got up when the alarm clock went off.
I had got up when the alarm clock went off.
I was getting up when the alarm clock went off.

Omitting *was* or *were* in sentences like:

They were walking along, enjoying each other's company, when . . .

(See *Practical English Usage* 468)

Relevant errors

☆ He was having three cups of tea when I arrived.
☆ I was knowing his name.
☆ We were hearing a crash while he did the washing up.
☆ There was a thunderstorm while the football match.
☆ It happened during they were playing football.

What were you doing?

AS A CLASS AND IN PAIRS

1 Discuss possible answers to the questions in the cartoons and talk about the differences in meaning. Allow students to make their own deductions and to ask any questions they may wish to.
2 The sentence writing phase is best done in pairs so that a collaborative set of answers is produced and there is some discussion about what may or

26

may not be correct in each case. Discuss the various versions and the differences in meaning. In the suggested model version below, many other variations may be possible.

He *had had* three cups of coffee when I arrived. *or had drunk*

She *opened* the door when she found her key.

I *was driving* along slowly when a dog ran into the road.

He *had read* nearly half the book when he fell asleep.

He *was changing* the baby when his wife got home. *or put the baby to bed*, etc.

I *was having* a cup of tea when the doorbell rang. *or had just had*, etc.

It might be worth pointing out to a higher level class that there are a number of verbs that are not normally used with the progressive form of the verb. These include such stative verbs as:

taste, hear, smell, etc.   *belong to, contain*, etc.
like, hate, love, etc.   *seem, appear*, etc.
believe, imagine, know, etc.

Yesterday

ALONE, THEN IN PAIRS OR GROUPS OF 3 OR 4

1 The first part of the activity should be done by each student working alone. Students with poor memories (or without watches) should estimate the various times and *not* leave any blanks.
2 Form groups of two to four students. Each student has to find out about the others' activities at various times yesterday.

➤ Extra activity

IN 3 GROUPS

The well-known, but ever popular, game 'Alibi' is best played by dividing the class into three groups and nominating three suspects who are sent out of the room to concoct an alibi for their movements between the hours of 10 am and 4 pm on Sunday, when the school was broken into and a valuable piece of audio-visual equipment stolen. Meanwhile the three groups decide what questions they are going to ask.

When the suspects are allowed back into the room, each of them is questioned by a different group (simultaneously) for five minutes or so. Then the suspects change groups and are interrogated by a different group for a further five minutes. Finally, if necessary, the suspects change groups again and are questioned by the last group.

After all the suspects have been questioned, the whole class compares its findings and decides whether the three suspects are possibly, probably or definitely guilty.

(This version of 'Alibi' was described by David Crookall in *Modern English Teacher* Vol. 7 No. 1.)

When the phone rang . . . 🖉

IN PAIRS

This exercise should be done collaboratively, as it is probably more difficult than it looks. Perhaps get the pairs to compare their sentences with another pair afterwards.

When the doorbell rang, *I was sitting at home watching TV.*

When the lights went out, *I was sitting in an armchair reading a good book.*

When the alarm clock went off, *I was lying in bed dreaming of my summer holidays.*

When my guests arrived, *I was standing in the kitchen preparing a meal.*

When I met my old friend, *I was walking in the park admiring the flowers.*

When the rain started, *I was lying on the beach enjoying the warm sunshine.*

When they called me for lunch, *I was sitting at my desk working very hard.*

I opened the curtains and . . . 🖉

As an introduction to the exercise, perhaps look at the picture together and get the class to identify each of the activities that were going on. The written work can be done as homework or, if there is time, in class.

5 PAST, PRESENT AND FUTURE

Summary

Practice in using the present perfect, present progressive and *going to* to talk about recent events, current events and imminent events:

She has walked out on her husband.   *She's walked out on him.*
She is thinking about her future.   *She's thinking about it.*
She is going to phone her friend.   *She's going to phone him.*

Using the simple past and *used to* to talk about activities that occurred in the distant past:

I once smoked 50 cigarettes a day.
Did you use to be a heavy smoker?
I used to smoke heavily.

Using the simple present to talk about current habits:

I don't smoke any more.
I only drink milk now.

Using *for* and *since* with the present perfect:

I haven't drunk spirits for 10 years.
I haven't drunk whisky since 1976.
I've been a teetotaller ever since I had the accident.

(See *Practical English Usage* 493, 494, 495, 472, 496, 497, 614)

Relevant errors

☆ What is happened?
☆ Don't you use to smoke a lot?
☆ I didn't smoke since three years.
☆ I haven't seen him since three years.
☆ I have been reading six pages so far.
☆ He still didn't do it yet.
☆ I have stopped smoking three years ago.
☆ I've been eating 14 sweets.
☆ I've eaten sweets for two hours.
☆ I am used to drink a lot of milk.

A woman alone

IN GROUPS OF 3 OR 4

Students should be encouraged to use their imaginations. To help them to do this, ask for one minute's silence for gazing and thinking before the groups are formed. Go from group to group during the conversation, making a note of the relevant errors you will point out later.

Get a spokesperson from each group to tell the others about the various theories.

(The Edward Hopper painting reproduced is 'Automat', 1927.)

What's going on?

IN PAIRS

Student A should look at activity 22, while student B looks at 32. A third student can share either A's or B's picture. Make sure everyone goes on to describe the events *before* and *after* their scenes.

What's happened?

AS A CLASS OR IN LARGE GROUPS

This activity can be done orally or in writing. It calls for several suggestions about each of the cartoon situations. Be alert for relevant errors and ask students to correct these themselves, if possible.

Those were the days

IN PAIRS

Make sure everyone understands what to do and, if necessary, set the scene more vividly ('Imagine that you're two old, old friends who haven't met for ages and you're amazed how much your lives have changed . . . ').

➡ **Extra activity**

IN PAIRS OR GROUPS OF 3 OR 4

Ask each pair or group to remember their own lives when they were several years younger: five or ten years ago, say. Get them to find out from each other what they used to do in those days, what they didn't use to do then that they do now, and how their lives have changed since then.

Before TV

IN GROUPS OF 4 OR 5

1 Students should ask each other similar questions to the ones shown beside the picture of the card-players. To begin with, ask for some suggested answers to those questions.
2 The written work may be set as homework. Perhaps ask students to write about just one aspect of their discussion.

6 SPELLING AND PRONUNCIATION

Summary

Saying aloud the letters of the alphabet when spelling out names or difficult words and understanding names which are spelt out at normal speed.

Recognising and using common homonyms:
break/brake, hole/whole, peace/piece, etc.

Spelling vowel sounds and diphthong sounds in different ways and pronouncing these correctly:
sheep ceiling easy even etc. (vowel sounds)
Eh? tray eight lazy grey paint etc. (diphthongs)

Doubling, or not doubling, consonants before -*ing*:
hoping, hopping, shopping, travelling, etc.

Spelling words with *ei* or *ie* correctly:
believe, receive, either, etc.

Correcting common spelling mistakes:
*allways, *wether, *aquaintance, etc.

(*Practical English Usage* 578, 568, 569, 570, 573, 574)

Relevant errors

Confusion between different letters of the alphabet ('Jones begins with G', 'Fifi ends with E', etc.).
Spelling mistakes (*allways, *wheather, etc.).
Pronunciation errors that result in misunderstanding.

➤→ Preliminary activity

AS A CLASS, THEN IN GROUPS OF 2 TO 4

1 To make sure everyone knows the letters of the alphabet and can understand them easily, spell out your own FULL NAME and FULL ADDRESS letter by letter and get the class to write them down.

2 Then, working in pairs or small groups, students spell out their own full names and addresses for their partner(s) to write down. Listen for confusion between *G* and *J*, *A* and *R*, *E* and *I*, etc.

What's in a name?

IN PAIRS

Student A should look at activity 17, while student B looks at 21. A third student can share A's information. The idea of this activity is to give practice in spelling aloud some difficult names and in understanding the spelling aloud. The listener has to write down the letters he or she hears and cope with the speed of delivery. Then, after a short time for guessing who's really who, the 'real' names of the famous people are revealed.

(The people in the photos are better known as Pelé, Marilyn Monroe and Omar Sharif. The names given in the communication activity are the real names of more people who are better known by their stage names or pseudonyms.)

Did you say 'court' or 'caught'?

IN GROUPS OF 3 OR IN PAIRS

Students have to discover each word's homonym and write the homonyms down. This activity introduces the problems of different spelling realisations of identical sounds in English.

brake *break*	meet *meat*	seen *scene*	wait *weight*
dew *due*	nose *knows*	shore *sure*	waste *waist*
flew *flu*	right *write/Wright*	steel *steal*	weather *whether*
guessed *guest*	root *route*	tale *tail*	week *weak*
hole *whole*	peace *piece*	threw *through*	wore *war*

The right answers to this exercise are in communication activity 46, so if any pairs find they can't cope, they can look there for reassurance.

A E I O U

IN PAIRS

This activity explores the different spelling realisations of English vowel sounds. Make sure the class are familiar with the phonetic symbols, which they must know if they want to use a dictionary efficiently – point this out if there is any resistance to the symbols.

Student A should look at activity 4, while student B looks at 20. A third student can share A's information. Each student has a secret list of words which he or she dictates to the partner, who has to write them down in the appropriate column. Make sure the members of each pair check each other's spelling.

'ei' or 'ie'?

IN PAIRS

The rule of thumb: 'I before E except after C' may not be very helpful, as this exercise shows. (Some accents of English might place *either* and *neither* in the /iː/ column.)

Eh? . . . Oh! . . . Ow!

IN PAIRS

Run through the phonetic symbols first. This activity explores different spelling realisations of diphthong sounds in English.

Student A looks at activity 10, while student B looks at 24. Allow time for the partners to check each other's spelling at the end.

Hoping or hopping?

IN PAIRS OR GROUPS OF 3

Check everyone's spelling at the end. (In American English the spellings *traveling*, *quarreling* and *kidnaping* are usual.)

➤→ Extra activity

AS A CLASS

Here are some 'difficult' words that commonly cause spelling problems. Dictate them to the class, saying each word twice, perhaps leaving out the ones your class will think are too easy:

accommodation	cupboard	foreign
happiness	pronunciation	resign
excitement	to practise	climb
judgement (judgment)	some practice	gauge
nuisance	treasure	access
sandwich	argument	address
handkerchief	wrist	awkward

Correct the mistakes

IN PAIRS

Provided that every mistake is spotted and corrected, there is no danger that students may get 'contaminated' by the incorrect forms. None of the mistakes in the exercise is as insidious as the ones that may have been made in the Extra activity above – apart from *to practice and *aquaintance, perhaps.

Whenever I'm not smiling, people allways ask me wether I'm feeling
deppressed or just a miserable sort of person. It's an awful nuisance
because no one can walk round grining on every occasion and I don't
beleive that basicly other people are any happyer than me. Psycholgists
(or do I mean psychyatrists ?) would probablly say that I'm lieing to
myself but I sincerely believe it's true. Althfough I try to practice
smiling in front of the mirror, it doesn't seem to have any affect. My
friends and aquaintances say, 'Come on, cheer up. It's not that bad!'

7 PUNCTUATION

Summary

Practice in using English punctuation accurately and appropriately:
> *When I found out, I was lost for words!*
> *It's very pleasant, isn't it?*
> *'Hallo, everybody!' he shouted to Tom, Dick and me.*

Using the correct name for each punctuation mark:
> *question mark, exclamation mark, hyphen, dash*, etc.

Recognising the meaning of different punctuation conventions:
> *My elder brother, who works in Japan, is 43.*
> *My sister who lives at home is 18 and the other one is 24 and is at college.*
> *It's wonderful?*
> *It's wonderful . . .*

Writing, understanding and saying aloud common abbreviations:
> *am, St, BBC, CUP*, etc.

Using capital letters appropriately:
> *January, Monday, Miss, Uncle Jim, English*, etc.

(*Practical English Usage* 505–510, 577)

Relevant errors

☆ She isnt here, is she?   ☆ She isn't here is she?   ☆ She isn't here, is she.
☆ Tell me all about it Bill.
☆ Tell me when I should come?
☆ I asked him, 'what's the time?'   ☆ I asked him, 'What's the time'?
☆ He speaks fluent japanese.
☆ I'll see you in july.
☆ Show me the word, which you don't understand.
☆ London which is on the Thames is the seat of government.

Say it aloud

IN PAIRS

1 First, make sure everyone can say the names of each punctuation mark:
question mark, exclamation mark, full stop (or period), comma, colon,
semi-colon, apostrophe, brackets (or parentheses), inverted commas (or
quotation marks), hyphen, dash.

2 Encourage everyone not to point at the errors, but to announce each of
them: 'The apostrophe should be before the *s* . . .'

Its nice today, isnt it? ✗	It's nice today, isn't it? ✓
Our cat's hurt its paw. ✓	Our cats hurt it's paw. ✗
He's a tall, dark, handsome man. ✓	He's a tall dark handsome man. ✗
She told me that she was sixteen. ✗	She told me that she was sixteen. ✓
If you want to see him make an appointment. ✗	If you want to see him, make an appointment. ✓
Make an appointment if you want to see him. ✓	Make an appointment if you want to see him. ✗
The person who phoned left this message. ✓	The person who phoned left this message. ✗
My mum, who is 62, never eats sweets. ✓	My mum who is 62 never eats sweets. ✗
My dad, on the other hand, has a sweet tooth. ✓	My dad on the other hand has a sweet tooth. ✗
That's right he said. ✗ "That's right!" he said. ✓	"That's right," he said. ✓

Excuse me, please.

IN PAIRS OR IN GROUPS OF 3

This exercise is best done collaboratively as there are a large number of
missing punctuation marks to find. To be helpful, you could announce that
there are 40 missing altogether.

There may be some discussion about commas and this may be a good time
for you to point out that the use of commas (and dashes, colons, semi-colons
and even full stops) is quite flexible in English – much more flexible than in
many other languages.

Man:	Excuse me, please.
Woman:	Yes, can I help you, sir?
Man:	I'd like to know when the Paris flight gets here.
Woman:	Which flight do you mean: the British Airways flight or the Air France one?
Man:	It's the British Airways, I think, because the flight number is BA 144.
Woman:	OK, I'll check for you if you'd just wait a moment. Yes, the scheduled arrival time is 1900 but there's a delay of 30 minutes.

⟫→

Man: Oh,I see,fine,thank you.Is there likely to be any further delay,do you think?
Woman: No,the plane's already on its way so,unless there's a headwind or
           something,it's probably going to land at about 1930.
Man: Right,thanks very much for your help.
Woman: You're welcome,sir.Goodbye.
Man: Bye.

---

etc.

IN GROUPS OF 3 OR 4

If your students are unfamiliar with most of the abbreviations, go through
them as a class before the groups test each other's memories. Note that some
familiar concepts, such as EEC or VAT, may have different abbreviations in
your students' language(s).

am	in the morning	St	Street (or Saint)
pm	in the afternoon or evening	Rd	Road
mph	miles per hour	Ave	Avenue
b & b	bed and breakfast	Sq.	Square
h & c	hot and cold running water	Dept	Department
max.	maximum	VAT	value added tax
min.	minimum	LP	long-playing record (album)
approx.	approximately	UN	United Nations
intro.	introduction	UK	United Kingdom
tel.	telephone number	CUP	Cambridge University Press

BBC	British Broadcasting Corporation
EEC	European Economic Community (The Common Market)
HQ	headquarters
GMT	Greenwich Mean Time
PTO	please turn over (the page)

▶→ Extra activity

AS A CLASS

Look together at the front page of an English-language newspaper, preferably
a 'serious' one with plenty of text and not too many photos and large head-
lines. Pick out the abbreviations and acronyms used and decide what they all
mean and how they are pronounced. Most acronyms (NATO, UNESCO,
IATA, etc.) are said as words, not as initial letters.

CAPITAL LETTERS

IN PAIRS OR GROUPS OF 3

Groups who claim to have finished first should be asked to check whether they have in fact made all the 21 necessary changes.

I'll see you on(f)riday or at the weekend, (m)r(j)ones.
If we don't meet in the summer, let's meet in(s)eptember or at(c)hristmas.
This is(u)ncle(f)ed who's in the(r)oyal(a)ir(f)orce.
I saw a programme about the sun and the moon on(tv)last night.
Most(s)cottish people prefer to call themselves(s)cots – unlike the whisky which is always called scotch. And the(hq)of the(m)etropolitan(p)olice is called(s)cotland(y)ard, which is in(l)ondon.
Now that he's a doctor, the name plate on his door says '(d)r(s)wan'.

Dear Mr Brown,

This exercise will need some preliminary work in class if the layout of the letter is likely to cause any problems. The written work can be done collaboratively in class or set as homework.

The model version shown below contains one or two optional changes to the original – different people and firms have their own styles of laying out letters.

```
                                  108 Alma Road
                                  Bournemouth
                                  BH9 1AL
                                  14 April 1985
Dear Mr Brown,

        I'm writing to you to let you know that I'll be away from school
until Monday next.  I'm sorry I couldn't let you know in person but your
secretary told me you were busy, so I didn't want to disturb you.

The reason for my absence is that my uncle from the United States is paying us
an unexpected visit and as I'm the only one in the family who speaks English,
I'm going to have to look after him.

If I had known sooner, I'd have told you but, as I said, the visit is
unexpected.

                    Yours sincerely,

                    Maria Garcia, Class B 13
```

8 POSITION: Place

Summary

Practice in using prepositions and prepositional phrases to describe location:

in, on, at, behind, in front of, beside, between, among, in the corner of, underneath, under, on the left of, etc.

Identifying position precisely:

It's half-way down the page, just to the right of . . .
They're above and slightly behind . . .
It's on the left-hand side, immediately below . . .

(*Practical English Usage* 484, 4, 88, 125, 50, 102, 248)

Relevant errors

☆ It's in middle of the line.   ☆ He's sitting at a chair.
☆ It's on left of the house.   ☆ He's sitting before the fire.
☆ It's between the trees in the forest.   ☆ It's among the two trees.
Imprecise or misleading use of prepositions and prepositional phrases.

Mouse trouble

AS A CLASS

This introductory exercise calls for precise identification of positions. Make sure that everyone puts a little circle ◯ round each mouse in the picture as it is identified by a member of the class.

When all 32 (or more?) mice have been spotted and encircled, tell the class exactly where you want them to put 12 mousetraps and get them to mark each position with a small M.

➤ **Extra activity**

AS A CLASS

Describe the 'diagram' which follows to the class step by step, and get them to draw the details as you give them. Do not tell anyone what the diagram represents, but make them rely on the precision of your description. Allow questions in case you haven't made yourself clear at any stage. Begin like this:

'*Draw a large square. Inside the square, filling most of the area, draw an oval or egg shape. Draw a wiggly line round the bottom part of the oval. Draw two half circles on the left and right of the oval, both outside it with their points touching the edge of the oval . . .*'

Refer to every item as a line, dot or circle, *not* as a nose, eyes or ears! (This activity is a lot harder than it looks, by the way.)

Where are the mistakes?

AS A CLASS AND THEN IN GROUPS OF 3

1   Ask for different suggestions on other ways to describe the location of each of Mr Jones's children. For example, the son in the distance is '*to the left of the shed and some way away*' or '*50 metres away from the shed*' etc.

   To encourage precise identification of positions, expressions like the following may be useful:

   quite near
   a few centimetres/inches/miles away from
   half-way between
   two thirds of the way
   just over half-way from
   exactly opposite

2   Keen eyesight is required for this exercise in 'proof-reading'. Allow time for the groups to spot all the misprints before asking the whole class to identify them all. The idea is not to just point to each misprint, but to say

41

exactly where it is. For example: *'There's a large space in the headline between FROM and FUNDS'* and *'At the end of the third paragraph the date is wrong.'* Identify any misprints the class haven't managed to spot.

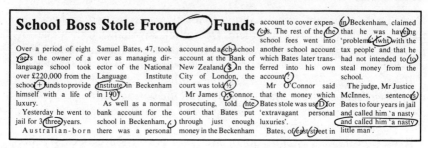

School Boss Stole From Funds

Over a period of eight yaes the owner of a language school took over £220,000 from the school funds to provide himself with a life of luxury.

Yesterday he went to jail for 3 three years. Australian-born Samuel Bates, 47, took over as managing director of the National Language Institute in Beckenham in 190.

As well as a normal bank account for the school in Beckenham, there was a personal account and a sch school account at the Bank of New Zealand in the City of London, the court was told.

Mr James O'Connor, prosecuting, told court that Bates put through just enough money in the Beckenham account to cover expences. The rest of the he school fees went into another school account which Bates later transferred into his own account.

Mr O'Connor said that the money which Bates stole was used for 'extravagant personal luxuries'.

Bates, of east street in Beckenham, claimed that he was having 'problems whi with the tax people' and that he had not intended to to steal money from the school.

The judge, Mr Justice McInnes, sentences Bates to four years in jail and called him 'a nasty and called him 'a nasty little man'.

Where shall I put A?

IN PAIRS

Each student begins by secretly scattering his or her half of the alphabet over the map. Then they must add their partner's letters to their own map in exactly the places described. Exact identification of the places is called for and understanding of this is tested as each letter is added to the map.

➤→ Extra activity

AS A CLASS

Describe the sketch below to the class, while they draw the details according to your instructions. No special artistic skills are required. (You may prefer to use a more complicated sketch of your own devising if you think your students need more of a challenge.)

What does it look like?

Student A looks at activity 14, while student B looks at 27. Each has a sketch which must be described to their partner so that the partner can draw a reasonably similar version. Perhaps reassure them that no special artistic skills are needed, provided that the instructions are detailed enough. Asking questions will help the listener to get a clearer idea of what the speaker is describing.

Fill in the gaps

This exercise can also be set as homework, but note that there are a number of places where several variations are possible and these will need to be discussed afterwards. The model version below is not definitive and your students may well have some better ideas which will provide some discussion.

So there I was, standing alone *on top of* the mountain looking *at* the view. I was *surrounded* by snow-capped peaks and could see the sun starting to set *in the west.* Slowly a red glow spread *across* the sky, making the *distant* peaks look pink, until the sun finally dropped *below* the horizon. Soon it would be quite dark and I could see grey clouds *in the sky* and could feel a chill *in* the air. It would have been foolish to stay *at the summit* much longer and I started walking *down* the slope towards the mountain hotel, which was half an hour's walk *away.* I was going to spend the night *there.* Sure enough, it began to snow and I realised that the path *between* the rocks would soon be *covered.* I started to run, not wanting to get lost *on* the mountain. I stopped *beside* a tree for a moment and saw the hotel *below* me. Of course I got there easily, but the next day the snow was so *thick* that we all stayed *inside,* singing songs *around* the fire.

9 POSITION: Direction and motion

Summary

Practice in using prepositions and prepositional phrases to describe direction of movement and changes of direction:
> *towards, away from, under, onto, into, off, over, round, between, past, to the left of, up, down,* etc.

Describing routes:
> *turn left at . . . , go straight on past . . . , go round . . .*
> *When you get to . . . , When you've passed . . .*

Using different verbs of motion with adverbial particles:
> *walk past, run down, fall over, creep along, fly around, jump up and down,* etc.

(*Practical English Usage* 7, 8, 448, 491, 492)

Relevant errors

☆ He walked away the house.
☆ He ran passed the school.
☆ He jumped off the wall.
☆ They jumped above the stream.

☆ She came out the building.
☆ She ran out of.
☆ It went left of the trees.
☆ Turn left and then go straight.

Trouble with mosquitoes

AS A CLASS

This exercise introduces different prepositions and prepositional phrases that indicate direction. Several interpretations of the arrows are possible! (This activity can be supplemented by pretending that one of the mosquitoes is at large in the classroom. Follow it round with your finger as it buzzes in different directions. Whenever it stops, students should shout out where they think it's going to next.)

Where did it go?

AS A CLASS

Starting at the top right-hand corner, explain to the class where the creature went. They should draw in the route as you explain it to them.

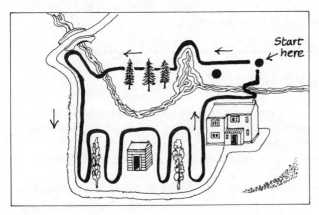

Go straight on until . . .

IN PAIRS

Student A should look at activity 11, while B looks at 57. A third student can either share A's information or just listen and draw both the cartoons. Each student describes a different 'route' round, among and between the numbers to their partner, who has to draw the route according to the instructions. The results become amusing cartoons.

Make sure everyone draws on their blank grid on page 18, not over their own cartoon in the communication activity.

This way please!

IN GROUPS OF 3, THEN IN PAIRS

After each group has decided on the best route from Union Station to include all of the sights, form pairs consisting of members of different groups. The members of each pair must describe their group's route as their partner adds it to their map. The routes must be described and *not* shown by pointing – make this 'rule' clear to everyone.

➤→ **Extra activity**

Use a large map of your own city or town. Decide together what the Top Ten tourist attractions are and then agree on a route between them for another elderly relative who insists on walking but who suffers from bad feet. The route should start and end in your classroom.

Run, walk or fly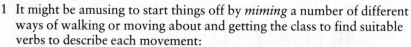

1 It might be amusing to start things off by *miming* a number of different ways of walking or moving about and getting the class to find suitable verbs to describe each movement:

stroll, creep, tiptoe, stride, hop, limp, stagger, crawl, march, etc.

Then ask for more ideas that you haven't been able to mime.

2 The sentence writing can be done collaboratively or set as homework. Many variations are possible and the model sentences below are simply suggestions:

As the stream was quite narrow, we managed to jump over.
As soon as he saw the tiger, he started to run away.
It looks as if he's just about to fall in.
She walked up and down, waiting for someone to come out.
He waved at me as he drove past.
The sun was shining brightly as they walked along.
There was so much traffic in the road that he couldn't get across.
The General saluted as the soldiers marched past.

10 DOING THINGS: Requests and obligation

Summary

Making requests:
>Would you mind doing this?   I'd like you to do this.
>Could you do this?   I want you to do this.
>Can you do this, please?   Please will you do this?

Asking for permission:
>Would you mind if I did this?
>Do you mind if I do this?
>May I do this?
>Could I do this?
>Is it all right if I do this?

Asking questions and making statements about prohibition and lack of prohibition:
>Can I do that?
>Am I allowed to do that?
>Is it all right to do that?

>You can't do that.   You can do that.
>You aren't allowed to do that. You're allowed to do that.
>You aren't supposed to do that. It's all right to do that.
>You mustn't do that.   If you like you can do that.

Asking questions and making statements about obligation and lack of obligation:
>Do I have to do that?
>Have I got to do that?
>Do I need to do that?
>Ought I to do that?
>Is there any need to do that?

>You have to do that.   You don't have to do that.
>You've got to do that.   You needn't do that.
>You ought to do that.   There's no need to do that.
>It's wise to do that.   You haven't got to do that.

(*Practical English Usage* 131, 132, 376, 394, 387, 363, 285, 586, 40, 447, 550, 399, 400)

Relevant errors

☆ Would you mind to open the door? ☆ I musted to do it.
☆ Need I to do it?   ☆ You needn't to do that.
☆ You don't can do that here. ☆ You don't have to doing that.

Would you mind . . . ?

IN GROUPS OF 3 AT FIRST

Give each group time to think how they would express the ideas. Then call
for suggestions from the class and correct any errors. With such structures
appropriacy is extremely important too, but for the purpose of this exercise,
it can be assumed that one is speaking to an acquaintance. Then, later, the
whole exercise can be gone through again with the class suggesting how they
would express the same ideas if they were talking to a close friend *or* to an
(older) stranger. The focus is on accuracy in this exercise, but if further
practice in appropriacy is called for, there is ample material in *Functions of
English** units 3 and 7.

*By Leo Jones, published by Cambridge University Press.

I'd like you to . . .

IN PAIRS

Student A should look at activity 8, while student B looks at 19. A third
student could share A's information or form a pair with the teacher. Each
student has to perform a series of actions, following his or her partner's
instructions, which may involve standing up, raising arms and closing eyes.
Nothing energetic (or improper) is called for, but if there is unused space
anywhere in the room it might be a good idea to move a cramped pair into it.

Make yourself at home?

IN GROUPS OF 3 OR PAIRS

Look at the suggested structures at the bottom of the page first and, if necessary, explain that there is a difference between things you're not allowed to do and things you're not supposed to do. In many cases this difference is insignificant in normal conversation, however.

Students without parents, or recently bereaved, may prefer to imagine a stereotyped 'grandparents' house'. As they work together, the members of the group may find themselves forming a composite image of a typical strict home.

Call for each group to announce its advice to the rest of the class.

Enjoy your flight!

IN GROUPS OF 3 OR 4

1 After the groups have decided on their answers, and committed themselves by putting ticks or crosses, ask them to tell the class their decisions:
'*You can't take a dog onto a plane, not even a small dog.*'
'*You're certainly allowed to take a briefcase on board.*'
'*Yes, but if you've already got a large handbag, you're not allowed to have a briefcase as well.*'
2 Follow a similar procedure before . . .
3 . . . allowing everyone to look at the right answers in activity 7. Give them time to talk about the mistakes they made.

Do I have to . . . ?

IN GROUPS OF 3 OR 4

If necessary, point out that there is a difference between things one ought to do and things one has to do or which it is wise to do. In normal conversation these differences are not always significant.

To start things off, remind the class how strange it feels to set foot in a foreign country for the first time: not just the unfamiliar language, but the climate, the habits of the people, the traffic and the public transport system all make one feel that one has set foot on a different planet. Things that a native takes for granted are often puzzling, not to say dismaying, for a newly-arrived visitor from abroad.

Allow time for an exchange of ideas at the end.

▶→ **Extra activity**

AS A CLASS

Prepare slips of paper with the names of different occupations:
    painter, Prime Minister, pop singer, priest, policeman, gardener, etc.
Get one member of the class to choose a slip secretly and at random. He or
she has to pretend that this is his or her real job. The others have to ask
questions beginning:

Can you . . . ?	*Do you have to . . . ?*
Are you allowed to . . . ?	*Have you got to . . . ?*
Are you supposed to . . . ?	*Are you expected to . . . ?*

to find out the occupation. Only *Yes* or *No* answers are allowed.

Allow time for several rounds of the game or, after one or two rounds as a
class, divide up into groups and continue the game in groups with the remaining
slips of paper shared between the groups and passed on after use.

In other words

This can be done collaboratively in pairs or set as homework.

In class you mustn't chew gum.	You aren't *allowed/supposed to chew gum.*
Is it necessary to attend every lesson?	Do I *have to attend every lesson?*
Can I bring my pet dog into class?	Is *it all right to bring my pet dog into class?*
Open your books at page 13.	I'd *like you to open your books at page 13.*
You don't have to wear a suit.	There's *no need to wear a suit.*
Could I leave early today?	Would *you mind if I left early today?*
Could you give these books out?	Would *you mind giving these books out?*
Exams are not compulsory.	You don't *have to take an exam.*

11 DOING THINGS: Ability

Summary

Asking questions and making statements about ability and inability:

Can you . . . ?	*I can't . . .*
Do you know how to . . . ?	*I'm unable to . . .*
I can . . .	*I wish I could . . .*
I'll be able to . . .	*It'd be nice to be able to . . .*

I was able to . . .	*I wasn't able to . . .*
I managed to . . .	*I didn't manage to . . .*
I succeeded in -ing . . .	*I didn't succeed in -ing . . .*
	I couldn't . . .

Describing how one would get help to do things:
I'd need someone to help me to . . .
I'd get someone to . . .
I'd have that done for me.

(*Practical English Usage* 128)

Relevant errors

☆ John could catch the bus yesterday.
☆ I don't can do that.
☆ I was able to do that by my own.
☆ I have done that by a mechanic.

☆ He managed doing it.
☆ I got someone cutting my hair.
☆ She succeeded to do it.
☆ Could you get the carrots yesterday?

Evening classes

IN PAIRS

Begin by deciding as a class what the person in the cartoons is saying or thinking at each stage shown.

This rather mechanical exercise introduces the different forms used to talk about ability and inability. As a safety check it might be wise to ask students to write down at least one set of sentences using the structures shown.

51

▶→ **Extra activity**

IN AN EVEN NUMBER OF SMALL GROUPS

Ask the members of each group to devise a questionnaire to find out about the abilities of the members of another group. Give examples of the kind of questions they could ask to get the required information:

COOKING: *Can you bake a cake? cook a soufflé? cook an omelette?*
DRIVING: *Can you drive a car? a van? a bus?*
RIDING: *Can you ride a horse? a motorbike? a camel?*
CLIMBING: *Can you climb over a fence? up a tree? up a cliff?*
ATHLETICS: *Can you run 100m? 1,000m? 100km?*
etc.

When the groups have composed an interesting, varied set of questions, the groups all combine to form double-size groups and ask each other the questions. The answers should be noted down so that reports can be given to the rest of the class later:

'All of them can ride a horse, one of them can ride a motorbike and three of them can't ride either a motorbike or a camel.'

Shopping lists

IN PAIRS

Student A looks at activity 2, while student B looks at 13. Each student has a different shopping list with notes on what he or she couldn't get or was able to get. The idea is for students to ask each other questions like:

Did you manage to get . . . ?
Were you able to get . . . ?

But not to ask:

Could you get . . . ? in this context, nor to answer:
I could get . . .

Make sure everyone is aware that *could* is not normally used to refer to the past, though *couldn't* is.

Success at last! 📝

IN PAIRS

1 Encourage the use of all the structures shown. After the exercise has been done, get each pair to compare their sentences with another pair.

2 In case inspiration fails, remind students that even catching a bus can be considered as a 'success' and forgetting to do one's homework a kind of 'failure'!

Do-it-yourself?

IN GROUPS OF 3 OR 4

Start the ball rolling by telling the class some of the things in the list that you are skilful enough to be able to do yourself, and some which you have to employ experts to do for you at considerable expense.

In other words

This exercise can be set as homework or done collaboratively in class.

He managed to swim across the river.
They were unable to leave the country.
She succeeded in finishing her work in time.
He didn't manage to get away from the police.
She's capable of playing any tune on the piano by ear.
She couldn't understand what I meant.
She got her mother to make the wedding cake.
You need a very good mechanic to repair your car.
I'm going to have my hair cut tomorrow.

12 DOING THINGS: Advice and suggestions

Summary

Asking for advice or suggestions:

Should I . . . ?   *Do you think I should . . . ?*
Is it worth -ing . . . ?   *Do you think it's worth -ing . . . ?*
Would it be a good idea to . . . ?   *Do you think it would be a good idea to . . . ?*

Is there any point in -ing . . . ?   *Do you think there's any point in -ing . . . ?*

I can't decide whether to . . .
I can't make up my mind whether to . . .
I'm wondering whether to . . .

Giving advice or making suggestions:

If I were you I'd . . .   *If I were you I wouldn't . . .*
I think you ought to . . .   *I don't think you ought to . . .*
Why don't you . . . ?   *It isn't a good idea to . . .*
I'd advise you to . . .   *I wouldn't advise you to . . .*
It'd be best to . . .   *It'd be better not to . . .*
You'd better . . .   *There's no point in . . .*
My advice would be to . . .
It's time you did that.

(*Practical English Usage* 553, 606, 275, 447, 635)

Relevant errors

☆ Is it worth to do that?
☆ If I were you I'll do that.
☆ Why you don't do that?
☆ You'd better to do that.
☆ It's time you do that.
☆ There's no point to do that.
☆ You'd better doing that.
☆ You better do that.
☆ Do you think should I do that?
☆ Do you think is it worth doing?

What should I do?

IN PAIRS

This exercise can be done partly or wholly in writing. It introduces the
grammatical problems involved in using different structures to ask for advice
– particularly those concerned with the gerund and infinitive. If preferred,
start as a class by asking students to finish each of the questions shown as if
the man in the cartoon were speaking:
'*Would it be a good idea to wait for the bus?*'
'*Is it worth going by bike?*'   etc.

If I were you . . .

AS A CLASS

Ask the class to suggest pieces of advice they might give to Joe in the cartoon.
Continue by mentioning that Joe also:
keeps arriving late for work   *sleeps badly*
only eats eggs and beans   *has dirty shoes*
spends every evening in a bar   *is unfit*

There's no point in . . .

IN GROUPS OF 3 OR 4

First, perhaps, as a class, make sure everyone can use the structures listed
accurately. Maybe point out that there are some differences between the
structures listed in the previous exercise and that, for example, *You'd better
not* . . . is an acceptable form but is more normally used for issuing warnings
than giving advice.

➡ Extra activity

IN AN EVEN NUMBER OF PAIRS, THEN IN GROUPS OF 4

Write up on the board a list of at least 10 countries that your students may
have visited or may know something about. In a multi-national class include
the countries represented in the class. Ask the pairs to choose the six countries
they'd advise people to visit if they have the chance and then to decide on one
city or region within each country which is worth going to *and* one city or
region that's not worth going to if one's time is limited.

When they're ready, combine the pairs to form groups of four. The members of the groups then advise the others which places to go to and which not to bother visiting:

> '*If I were you I wouldn't go to Ireland, but I'd certainly go to France. And there's no point in going to the Riviera if your time's limited. It'd be best to go to Paris . . .*'

The list you put up would be based on your students' experience, but the one here is given to show what might be done. Handwritten beside each country are the places a pair of students might think of that might be worth visiting or not.

```
GERMANY  ✗
IRELAND  ✗
FRANCE   ✓  Paris ✓  Riviera ✗
BRAZIL   ✓  Rio ✓  Amazon jungle ✗
GREECE   ✓  Athens ✓  Crete ✗
JAPAN    ✓  Tokyo ✗  Kyoto ✓
etc.
```

That's easier said than done

IN GROUPS OF 4

Allow enough time in this role-play activity for each member of the group to have a turn and receive advice from the others. Encourage them to reject unsuitable or unrealistic advice and to ask 'How can I do that?' – not to accept the first solution offered!

If any of the problems are solved too quickly, here are some further suitable ones:

> '*I'm getting very bored with life.*'
> '*I'm getting too fat.*'
> '*I don't know what I'm going to do when this course is over.*'
> '*I can't decide what career I'm going to take up.*'

People with problems

Perhaps begin with a short preliminary discussion so that a number of different solutions can be generated. Does everyone agree what Liz's problem is? The writing can be done collaboratively in class, or set as homework.

Let everyone look at one or two other people's letters and comment on the advice given.

13 VERB + VERB: *-ing* and *to* . . .

Summary

Units 13, 14 and 15 cover all the main problems associated with the use of the gerund and the infinitive, including verbs that may be followed by the gerund and/or the infinitive and/or a *that* . . . clause

This unit gives practice in using the gerund or the infinitive in sentences like:
Going abroad is pleasant.   *It's pleasant to go abroad.*
Being punished is horrid.   *It's horrid to be punished.*
Playing football can be dangerous.   *It can be dangerous to play football.*

Using the gerund after a preposition:
I did it without holding on.
I did it by gripping with my elbows.

Using verbs normally followed only by the gerund:
avoid, carry on, detest, enjoy, finish, etc.

Using verbs normally followed only by the infinitive:
choose, learn, manage, mean, need, etc.

Using verbs that can be followed by either the gerund or the infinitive, without significant change in meaning:
begin, start, intend, continue, etc.
(Slight differences in meaning are ignored, as they are of little relevance to students who are below Proficiency level or equivalent.)

(*Practical English Usage* 319, 322, 334, 336, 339, 124)

Relevant errors

☆ To go on holiday is fun.
☆ He avoided to do it.
☆ She expected doing it.
☆ I can't sneeze without to close my eyes.
☆ I enjoy to watch football.

It's easy to . . .

IN PAIRS

1 This exercise should be done collaboratively, then each pair can show their questions to another group or ask them the questions and get them to give their answers or, perhaps, perform some of the actions.
2 Perhaps add *It's fun* and *It's easier to . . . than to . . .* or *It's harder to . . . than to . . .* to the list. Allow time for each pair to announce their best sentences to the class, or to show them to another pair.

Without blinking

IN PAIRS

This exercise should be done collaboratively, then each pair can show their questions to another group or ask them the questions and get them to give their answers or, perhaps, perform some of the actions.

The suggested model version below is not intended to be definitive and many variations are possible:

Can you sneeze without *closing your eyes?*
Can you stop hiccups by *drinking a glass of water slowly?*
Can you cure a cold by *taking medicine?*
Can you write a letter in English without *making any mistakes?*
Can you touch your toes without *bending your knees?*
Can you stand on one leg while *swinging your arms round?*

-ing or *to* . . . ?

Allow a few moments' silence for study. Then make sure everyone understands the verbs shown. Encourage questions in case anyone is unsure about how to use any of the verbs.

In other words

ALONE OR IN PAIRS

Compare the completed sentences and check on accuracy.

He was pretending to be a policeman.

We can't afford to buy that new TV.
I dislike watching TV every evening.
I'm going to put off writing until tomorrow.
Don't risk swimming here.
I hesitate to criticise your performance.
The parcel failed to arrive.
I'm waiting to see the doctor.
You should give up smoking.

I prefer . . .

IN PAIRS OR GROUPS OF 3

1 Allow time for questions.

2 Compare completed sentences.

> *He loves playing football.*
> *He started playing when the whistle blew.*
> *He hates washing up.*
> *I intend to go on holiday to Spain.*
> *She began to feel better after taking her medicine.*

3 To arouse enthusiasm for this activity, mention some of your own pet
  hates, loves and likes:
> '*I love watching football but I hate playing it.*'
> '*I enjoy eating good food but I dislike cooking.*'
> '*I like to drive a car but I hate being a passenger.*'
(Perhaps point out that although one can say both *I like doing it* and *I like
to do it*, the forms *I'd like to do it* or *Would you like to do it?* are the only
ones possible.)

➤→ Extra activity

AS A CLASS

To help everyone remember, and to test their memories, go through the verbs
that have come up in this unit and get the class to shout out 'doing it' or 'to
do it':
Teacher: I can't afford . . .
Class: TO DO IT!!

Finish the sentences

This invention exercise may be harder than it looks. Unimaginative students may need a partner's help if they are to write more than just *doing it* or *to do it*, which are not allowed in this exercise!

The model answers below are merely suggestions and not definitive:

Their dog is so fierce that I'd never dare *to go in their garden.*

After answering the phone he continued *to watch the programme.*

I've got such a bad cold that I can't help *coughing and sniffing.*

Please carry on working, I really don't mind *waiting for you to finish.*

While she's so far away from home she misses *being with her family.*

I dislike Bill so much that I always try to avoid *talking to him.*

While I was in town the day before yesterday I happened *to see my ex-husband.*

During the next twelve months I expect *to visit Germany.*

14 VERB + VERB: *-ing, to* . . . and *that* . . .

Summary

Using the infinitive or *that* . . . in sentences like:
    It seems to be here.   *It seems that it is here.*
    It appears to be true.   *It appears that it is true.*
    It is thought to be difficult.   *It is thought that it is difficult.*
    It is believed to be easy.   *It is believed that it is easy.*

Using different forms of the infinitive:
    to do   *to be doing*
    to have done   *to be done*

Using verbs that are normally only followed by an object and the infinitive:
    encourage someone to do something, force someone to do something, etc.

Using verbs that are normally only followed by *that* . . . :
    hear that someone has done something, assume that something has
    happened, etc.

Using verbs that can be followed by either the infinitive or *that* . . . :
    He's pretending to be stupid.   *He's pretending that he's stupid.*
    He decided to do it.   *He decided that he would do it.*

Using verbs that can be followed either by an object and the gerund or
that . . . :
    I found him doing it.   *I found that he was doing it.*
    I noticed them watching me.   *I noticed that they were watching me.*

(*Practical English Usage* 339, 323, 334, 544, 339, 124)

Relevant errors

☆ He seems liking animals.   ☆ I noticed him to do it.
☆ He encouraged me doing it. ☆ I taught him doing it.
☆ He assumed me to do it.   ☆ I seem to lost my Access card.
☆ The milk seems to boil over! ☆ I expect failing the exam.

He seems to . . .

IN PAIRS

Allow time for comparison and discussion of sentences at the end, making sure the different forms of the infinitive have been used correctly.

It appears that the window is broken. The window appears *to be broken.*

It seems that some of my books are missing. Some of my books seem *to be missing.*

It seems that none of my records have been touched. None of my records seem *to have been touched.*

It appears that nobody heard any suspicious noises. Nobody appears *to have heard any suspicious noises.*

It is thought that the thief is someone I know. The thief is thought *to be someone I know.*

It is believed that he knows me quite well. He is believed *to know me quite well.*

---

to . . . or that . . . ?

ALONE OR IN PAIRS

Call for silence while the verbs are studied. They will be used in the next exercise. Allow time for questions.

In other words

IN PAIRS

He thinks all strikers should be jailed.
She invited me to go dancing.
He found out that he hadn't got the job.
I bet you can't guess the answer.
I hope to see you next spring.
I dreamt I was being chased down a long corridor by a monster.
They were forced to go to bed early.
He got his secretary to make the call.
I felt that she didn't really like me.
I know that she won't come and see us today.

While I was out . . .

IN PAIRS

Students should work out how each sentence might finish, describing the children's behaviour, then compare their ideas with another pair. This could be done in writing.

While I was out I imagined *Timmy painting on the wall.*
When I got home I found *Oliver playing in my room.*
And then I discovered *Thomas spilling his drink all over the carpet.*
And noticed *Daniel using my typewriter.*
And believe it or not, I caught *Jeremy throwing biscuits all over the kitchen.*

A more advanced class could be informed at this stage of the very subtle difference between:
     I heard the wind blowing in the trees.
and   *I heard someone break a window.*
Or   *I saw Timmy interfering with my things.* (which took a little time)
and   *I saw Oliver draw on my book.* (which he did quickly)
   An intermediate class would certainly find this distinction confusing and pettifogging, as the difference in meaning is often very slight.
(See *Practical English Usage* 288)

▶→ Extra activity

AS A CLASS

To help everyone to remember the use of the verbs in this unit, go through them in a random order and get the students to call out: 'that he did it', 'him doing it' or 'him to do it':
Teacher: I assume . . .
Class: THAT HE DID IT.
   Perhaps include some of the more difficult verbs from unit 13, which should be followed by 'doing it' or 'to do it'.

Finish the sentences

As this kind of invention exercise may be harder than it looks, less imaginative students may need a partner's help. The exercise can be set as homework too.

You've won first prize? But I never realised *that you had entered.*
I can't find my keys. Will you please help *me to find them.*
I think she'd succeed if someone encouraged *her to work harder.*
What a lovely surprise! I didn't expect *to be given such a nice present.*
While you were sitting in the garden did you notice *anyone looking at you over the fence?*
As soon as I heard the phone ring I guessed *that it was you.*
After a long discussion they decided *to split up.*
He's such a bad teacher he couldn't teach *a monkey to eat a banana.*

15 VERB + VERB: *-ing* or *to* . . .?

Summary

This unit looks at some of the 'problem verbs' where the gerund and the infinitive have different meanings.

Using *stop* + gerund, *stop* + infinitive and *go on* + gerund:
  He stopped walking.   *He stopped to pick some flowers.*
  He went on walking.

Using *remember* and *forget* + gerund and + infinitive:
  I remember doing that.   *I remembered to do it.*
  I'll never forget doing it.   *I forgot to do it.*
  Do you remember doing that?   *Did you remember to do it?*

Using verbs + *to* + gerund:
  look forward to doing it, get used to doing it, become accustomed to doing it, object to doing it

Using *sorry* + *about* + gerund and *sorry* + *that* . . . :
  I'm sorry about breaking it.   *I'm sorry that I broke it.*

Using *let* and *make* + infinitive (without *to*) and *force* and *allow* + infinitive:
  They let me do it.   *They allowed me to do it.*
  They made him do it.   *They forced him to do it.*

Using the gerund as the subject of a sentence:
  Smoking is not allowed.   *Drinking is frowned upon.*

(*Practical English Usage* 339, 337, 320)

Relevant errors

☆ Please stop to annoy me.
☆ I'm sorry I forgot getting it.
☆ I'm looking forward to go there.
☆ I'm used to do work at home.
☆ I used to coming to school.

☆ I'm sorry to break it.
☆ They won't let me to do it.
☆ They made me to do it.
☆ We aren't allowed smoking.

Stop! [image]

IN PAIRS

Before starting the activity, make sure everyone understands the distinctions shown in the cartoons. Perhaps give further examples if necessary.

Student A should look at activity 33, while student B looks at 39.
In the first part, each student performs a series of annoying actions. His or her partner reacts by saying:
  '*Please stop sniffing*' or '*Please don't go on whistling*', etc.

In the second part, each student talks about a walk he or she went on, which involved a number of stops along the way. A conversation like the following develops:
A: Why did you make your first stop?
B: I stopped to pick a flower.
A: I see, and then what?
B: After picking the flower, I went on walking but I soon stopped again.
A: Why did you stop again?

At the end perhaps get everyone to write down some sample sentences to help them to remember.

Don't forget! [image]

IN PAIRS

This is a similar kind of communication activity. Again, make sure everyone understands the contrast shown in the cartoon.

Student A looks at activity 38, while B looks at 47.
In the first part each student has a list of things he or she is supposed to have remembered to do, some of which have been forgotten. A conversation like this develops:
A: Did you remember to phone the hairdresser?
B: No, I forgot to phone. Did you remember to buy some beer?
A: Yes I remembered to get it. Look, here it is!

In the second part each student casts his or her mind back to some unforgettable (real) experiences. A conversation about memories and never-to-be-forgotten events develops:
A: Do you remember going abroad for the first time?
B: Yes, I'll never forget landing at the airport and being stopped at the customs. What about you? What do you remember about your first date?
A: I remember feeling very nervous and . . .

A feedback session at the end may be necessary to clear up any confusions.

Looking forward to . . .

1 Make sure everyone understands that *to* is a preposition in this case and that prepositions are followed by the *-ing* form.
2 Once the five best pieces of advice have been written down, they can be shown to another group or discussed as a class.
Ask everyone what they are looking forward to doing in the near future and what they are not looking forward to doing.

➡️ Extra activity

A more advanced class may find it useful to look at the difference between:
    I tried to open the door but it was locked.
and *I tried banging on the door but nobody heard me.*
For example:
    'If you're locked inside a room what should you do? Well, first I'd try to attract someone's attention. But how? Well, I could try shouting or I could try rattling the door handle . . . '
Ask the class to suggest how you might solve the following problems:
    Being able to afford a holiday abroad
    Learning a new foreign language from scratch
    Improving your appearance
    Improving your terrible memory
    Becoming fit and slim

Sorry!

This exercise reinforces the rule that after a preposition only the gerund, or a noun phrase or a noun or pronoun can be used – never the infinitive:
    I'm sorry about breaking it.
    I'm sorry about what I've done.
    I'm sorry about the accident.
    I'm sorry about that.
    Point out that this rule applies to all the verb + preposition phrases (see units 27 and 28) and phrasal or prepositional verbs (see units 38 and 39).
    Note that we can also say: *I'm sorry for breaking it* and *I'm sorry to have broken it.*

⟫➜

*She's sorry about breaking them. And he's sorry that they're
    broken.*
I'm sorry about losing it. And you're sorry that I've lost it.
*He was sorry about spilling it. And she was sorry that he had
    spilt it.*
So he apologised for spilling it and ruining her dress.

Rules

IN GROUPS OF 3

Begin by getting students to imagine that they are unlucky enough to be
pupils at the school in question and that they are complaining about the
plethora of rules.

Afterwards get them to write down some of the rules.

Ask about the rules of the school or institute you're really in. What are the
(perhaps unstated but generally understood) rules of behaviour? Are they too
lax or too strict?

In other words

This exercise tests some of the verbs covered in this unit and should be done
alone or as homework.

I wish you wouldn't ask so many questions. Please stop *asking me
    questions.*
NO PARKING IN SCHOOL GROUNDS. We aren't allowed *to park in
    the school grounds.*
I think we need some petrol. We'd better stop *to get some petrol.*
We used to play cards every evening. I'll never forget *playing cards with
    you every evening.*
I've drunk your coffee by mistake. I'm sorry *about drinking your coffee.*
I get embarrassed when I meet strangers. I'm not used *to meeting
    strangers.*
I didn't tell you my phone number. I forgot *to tell you my phone
    number.*
I cough when I smoke a cigarette. Cigarettes make *me cough.*

16 THE FUTURE: Plans and intentions

Summary

This, the first of two units concerned with the future, looks at the grammatical forms used to describe plans, state intentions and talk about future activities in general.

Practice in using *will* or *going to* appropriately:
> *I'll see you tomorrow.* (promise)
> *I'm going to open this door.* (intention)
> *I'll open the door for you.* (offer)

Using the present progressive, present simple or *going to* appropriately:
> *I'm seeing the dentist first thing tomorrow.* (arrangement)
> *The train gets in at 17.35.* (timetable)
> *She's going to have a baby in September.* (certainty)

Using the present simple or present perfect (and not *will* or *going to*) in time clauses:
> *I'll make some coffee when they get here.*
> *We'll have tea when you've unpacked.*
> *I'll go for a walk if the sun starts shining.*

Using different verbs in reporting future plans and intentions:
> *promise, intend, offer, threaten,* etc.

The rules of usage can be terribly confusing, even for native speakers, and rule-giving is best avoided. For example, although the following sentences all mean more or less the same, there are very slight different shades of meaning:
> *I'm going to visit Athens on the 12th.*
> *I'll visit Athens on the 12th.*
> *I'm visiting Athens on the 12th.*
> *I visit Athens on the 12th.*

The bewildered student may find it more helpful to be given a rough-and-ready rule of thumb like this:
> 'If in doubt, use *going to* in speech and *will* in writing'

instead of getting bogged down in subtle shades of meaning.

(No distinction is made between *will* and *shall*, as the difference between them is unimportant in contemporary colloquial English.)

(*Practical English Usage* 250, 253, 536, 254)

Relevant errors

☆ I'll go there when the train will arrive.
☆ Everything is getting better soon.
☆ Everything gets better next week.
☆ If I'll pass my exam, I'll be happy.
☆ If I'm going to pass my exam, I'm going to be happy.

One day . . .

IN PAIRS OR ALONE

This exercise can be used to diagnose what difficulties your students may have with the forms that will be practised in this unit. The answers given below are merely suggestions and a myriad of different, equally suitable answers can be expected.

One of these days I'*m going to lose my temper with her*.
Tomorrow morning at 9.15 I'*m catching a plane to Italy*.
What presents *are you going to get* for your next birthday?
By the time the bus *arrives here* we'll all be wet through.
After work next Friday I'*ll go home and sit on the balcony*.
I'll *go and have a sandwich* when the bell rings.
Their plane *arrives at Heathrow* at 6 o'clock tomorrow morning.
As soon as I can I'*ll let you know my decision*.

One of the points that should be emphasised during this unit is that *will* and *going to* are often used synonymously, more or less. The same is true of *going to* and the present progressive in many cases too. See *Practical English Usage* for detailed rules of usage.

Reporting

IN PAIRS

This exercise shows how *will* or *going to* can be used to perform several different functions. It also provides a foretaste of units 19 and 20 on Reported Speech.

	Function	*Report*
'I won't* tell anyone about our secret.'	PROMISE	He promised not to tell anyone.
'I'm going to visit Italy next summer.'	INTEND	He intends to visit Italy.
'Will you help me to do this please?'	*ASK*	He asked me to *help him.*
'I think you'll* enjoy reading this book.'	*ADVISE*	*He advised me to read it.*
'Will* you be quiet!'	*TELL*	*He told me to be quiet.*
'I'm going to study hard for the exam.'	*INTEND*	*He intends to work hard for the exam.*
'I'll* hit you if you don't do what I say!'	*THREATEN*	*He threatened to hit me.*
'You'll* get cold if you forget your hat.'	*WARN*	*He warned me not to forget my hat.*
'I'll open the door.'	*OFFER*	*He offered to open the door.*
'I'm going to open the door.'	*INTEND*	*He intends to open the door.*
'I'll make you a lovely birthday cake!'	*OFFER*	*He offered to make me a lovely birthday cake.*

(*going to* can be used here, without much change in meaning.)

Correct the mistakes

IN PAIRS

This exercise gives examples of some 'typical' errors of usage. It also introduces the 'No *will* in a time clause' rule.

Make quite sure everyone has spotted all the errors and then corrected each of them.

⟫⟶

```
I'll make some tea when my friends w̶i̶l̶l̶ arrive.
```

The weather's ⁄gett̶i̶n̶g̶ better next week. *going to*

His sister⁄w̶i̶l̶l̶ have a baby the month after next. *is going to*

I think I⁄go out for a walk soon.   *'ll*

If they ̶'̶r̶e̶ ̶g̶o̶i̶n̶g̶ ̶t̶o̶ have enough money, they're going abroad this summer.

We won't catch the train if we⁄w̶o̶n̶'̶t̶ hurry. *don't*

➤→ **Extra activity**

AS A CLASS

To introduce different adverbial phrases that are used to refer vaguely to future time and also to give practice in using time clauses, pretend that you're thinking of visiting a number of different countries and cities in the near future. Responses like those shown below can be encouraged from several students each time.

Teacher: I'm thinking of going to Egypt in a year or two.
Student A: Oh really? If you go there, I expect you'll see the Pyramids.
Student B: Yes, and while you're there you'll probably have a look at the Aswan Dam.
Student C: If you go there, will you have time to visit Alexandria?
Student D: If you're in Egypt, will you go on a Nile cruise?

  I might go to London sooner or later.
  I'm probably going to New York the year after next.
  I thought I might go to Paris one day soon.
  I'm thinking of going to Brazil in a year or two.
  I was wondering about going to Switzerland in a few months' time.
  I'm off to Germany fairly soon.
  I'd like to go to Japan one of these days.
  I've booked up to go to Rome in ten days' time.
  I expect I'll be in Greece again before too long.
  I plan to go to Spain in a few years' time.
PLUS more countries or cities that your students know something about. If necessary, replace some of the places given with local cities or regions.

Consequences

IN GROUPS OF 3 OR 4

The members of the group should 'role-play' each sentence in turn, so that the others can react to each threat or intention. Encourage several different reactions to each of the sentences.

Planning ahead

ALONE FIRST, THEN IN PAIRS

1 Students with few plans or engagements should invent as many as necessary to fill their diaries up and give themselves a busier week.
2 Then, working in pairs, they discover each other's plans and suggest unforeseeable events that might jeopardise those plans:
  A: I'm taking the train to London on Tuesday morning.
  B: What will you do if the trains are on strike?
  A: Oh, well, if there's a train strike, I'll have to go by car.

Next summer . . . 🖾

IN PAIRS AT THE END

1 The written work can be done alone or in pairs in class. (If it is set as homework, leave time in class for part 2 below.)

Next summer I*'m going to* have a really good holiday. Of course, I*'ll* have to save up for it and do without some luxuries because otherwise I *won't be* able to afford it. I haven't decided where I*'ll* go yet. On the one hand it *would be* nice to go somewhere warm and sunny where I *could* lie on the beach all day, but on the other hand I *might* get bored with that and it *may be* better to choose a more active holiday. The important thing *is to* have a real change from routine. While I*'m* away, I*'ll* send you a postcard!

2 Begin by telling the class about your *own* summer holiday plans. Then get them to work in pairs (or groups of three) and tell each other about their holiday plans. Encourage detail, not just a short sentence:
  '*I'm going to stay with my uncle on his farm and most of the time I'll have to help with the work there. But I'll have some time to myself and then I'll be able to . . .* ' etc.
3 This could become a written composition if the activity interests enough students.

17 PROBABILITY

Summary

Practice in showing degrees of certainty, probability, possibility or uncertainty, improbability, and impossibility when talking about future events:

Certainty
I'm (absolutely) sure it'll ...
It's sure to ...
I'm quite sure it'll ...
It must be going to ...
It'll ..., that's for sure.

Probability
It'll probably ...
I expect it'll ...
It may well ...
It could well ...
It's likely to ...
It looks as if it'll ...
It seems to be going to ...

Possibility/Uncertainty
It may ...
It might ...
It could ...
There's a chance it'll ...

Improbability
It probably won't ...
I don't expect it'll ...
I doubt if it'll ...
It's unlikely to ...
It doesn't look as if it'll ...
It doesn't seem to be going to ...

Impossibility
I'm absolutely sure it won't ...
I'm quite certain it won't ...
It won't ..., that's for sure.
It can't be going to ...

Using the same structures to assess the truth of statements made about the present:

It's sure to be true.
I expect it's true.
It can't be true.
It may be true.
I'm quite certain it's not true.
etc.

Assessing the likelihood of events having happened in the past, using the same structures with the past simple or perfect infinitive.

I'm sure it happened.
It probably happened.
It can't have happened.
It's sure to have happened.
It must have happened.
etc.

(*Practical English Usage* 250, 251, 252, 377, 130)

Relevant errors

☆ It might happen yesterday.
☆ I'm sure it doesn't rain tomorrow.
☆ It might probably rain.

☆ It must be happen.
☆ It seems to be not going to rain.
☆ I'm absolutely sure it might not rain.

How sure are you?

AS A CLASS THEN IN GROUPS OF 3 OR 4

The expressions given in the Student's Book have been chosen because:
a) they can all be used to refer to future, present and past events and states, and
b) they are sources of grammatical errors or confusion.

Begin by making sure everyone can use the expressions accurately. Ask about the likelihood of various topical events happening in the near future. On the February day these notes were written, for example, questions like the following might have been asked:
Do you think Reagan will be re-elected?
Do you think the British couple will win the gold medal?
Is there going to be more snow tomorrow?
Will the new Soviet leader be more friendly to the West?
Ask similar questions about topics in the news currently.

Then arrange groups. Encourage each member of a group to suggest a *different* ending to each sentence. The best ideas should be written down and, later, announced to the rest of the class. Allow time for a short discussion of any controversial ideas.

Looking on the bright side?

IN PAIRS

To start the ball rolling, divide the class into Optimists and Pessimists and ask for their comments on the weather that might be expected in the next few days:

Optimists: *'It'll probably get warmer,' 'I doubt if it'll rain again tomorrow.'*
'It's sure to be sunny at the weekend.' etc.
Pessimists: *'It won't be fine on Sunday, that's for sure.' 'It's likely to snow this afternoon.' 'There may be heavy rain and flooding.'* etc.

Then get the pairs to work together and discuss each of the situations illustrated in the cartoons, still playing their roles. At the end find out which were the most blackly pessimistic and rosily optimistic ideas.

➤→ Extra activity

IN PAIRS

Use a set of large photos from magazines. Hold each one up for everyone to see and get each pair to speculate what the people in the photo are likely to do next. For example, a picture showing a couple having a meal might prompt comments like:

'It looks as if they're going to enjoy the meal.'
'The man may not have enough money with him to pay the bill.'
'It doesn't look as if she's going to . . .' etc.

Again, the best ideas can be written down.

Is it true?

IN PAIRS, THEN IN GROUPS OF 4

First of all, make sure that the examples on page 34 can be transformed easily:

(be going to) happen → be true
will happen   → is true
won't happen   → isn't true

Note also that It looks as if/doesn't look as if becomes It sounds as if/doesn't sound as if.

1 Encourage the invention of some plausible lies about, for example, some people they have met or places they have been to.
2 Combine the pairs into groups of four (and if necessary one group of six) for conversations like this to develop:

A: B once saw the Pope in Rome.
C: That doesn't sound as if it's true.
D: Well, it could be true, because B did go to Italy last year.
B: No, it's not true actually. I've only ever seen him on TV.

Did it happen?

IN GROUPS OF 3 OR PAIRS

1 Again, some transformations are needed to use the structures from page 34 to talk about past events:

(be going to) happen → have happened
will happen   → happened
won't happen   → didn't happen
etc.

2 Get each group to announce its best ideas to the rest of the class.

Why do you think . . . ?

IN PAIRS

Student A should look at activity 36, while student B looks at 41. Student A has to guess the reasons why Alex, Bob, Chris and David find (or found) themselves in the situations described – the other student has the right answers. Then student B has to guess why Emma, Frank, George and Hilda find (or found) themselves in some other situations – student A has the answers this time.

In other words

This can be done as homework or in class. The answers here are suggestions only:

I'm sure our train will be late.	Our train *is sure to be late.*
I probably won't see you tomorrow.	I doubt *if I'll see you tomorrow.*
I'm sure I wasn't told about the party.	I *wasn't told about the party, that's for sure.*
They seem to be a wonderfully happy couple.	I *expect they're wonderfully happy.*
It looks as if you've had a nasty shock.	You *seem to have had a nasty shock.*
This can't possibly be your handwriting.	This *definitely isn't your handwriting.*
You probably weren't careful enough.	It *looks as if you weren't careful enough.*

18 COMPARISON

Summary

Practice in using comparative and superlative forms of adjectives and adverbs:

good	*better*	*best*	*bad*	*worse*	*worst*
well	*better*	*best*	*badly*	*worse*	*worst*
fast	*faster*	*fastest*			

intelligent   more intelligent   most intelligent
happily   more happily   most happily

Talking about differences, using comparatives and superlatives:
Brazil is (much) larger than Greece.
Greece isn't (quite) as cold as Canada.
Canada is (much) less humid than Japan.
Japan is (much) more mountainous than Uruguay.
Uruguay is the flattest country in South America.
South America is the least populated continent of all, apart from Australasia.

Using *so, such a, too* and *enough* in result-clauses:
Cinderella's ugly sister's feet were so big that the slipper didn't fit.
She had such big feet that the slipper wouldn't go on.
It was such a small slipper that it wouldn't fit her foot.
The slipper wasn't large enough to fit her foot.
It was too small to go on her enormously fat foot.

(*Practical English Usage* 142, 143, 144, 145, 146, 147, 148)

Relevant errors

☆ Mine is gooder than yours.
☆ Mine is better as yours.
☆ Mine isn't as good than yours.
☆ Mine is more better than yours.
☆ It isn't easy enough that I can do it.
☆ It's such easy that I can do it.
☆ This is interestinger than that.
☆ It's the best of the world.

Braver than a lion!

IN GROUPS OF 4

This activity is designed to provoke disagreements within each group, and subsequently between the groups.

1 Get everyone to identify the creatures to their own satisfaction (including arguing whether the second animal is a wolf or a dog, or the third a mouse or a rat, etc.!). The list-making exercise can be speeded up or cut short if students are finding it too easy.

2 Do leave enough time for this part, which is more interesting and demanding.

More exciting than knitting!!

IN GROUPS OF 3 OR 4

Get everyone to give their *reasons* for deciding, for example, that skiing is more energetic than playing football. Don't spend too long on this activity if your class are doing it easily and accurately.

➤→ Extra activity

AS A CLASS

This game, a well-tried old favourite, extends the idea of the previous activities and acts as a lead-in to the next one. The idea is to state the various differences between everyday objects, using comparative sentences. For example, the difference between *a chair* and *a table* might be described as:

'*A table has longer legs than a chair.*'
'*A chair is more comfortable to sit on than a table.*'
'*A table is more convenient for eating off than a chair.*'

To make the game less predictable and more challenging, the use of
bigger, larger, taller and *smaller* or *shorter*
can be forbidden.

Here are some ideas to choose from and to supplement with your own ideas:

carpet – mat	gate – door	fence – wall
chocolate – toffee	ice cream – ice lolly	cash – credit cards
bank – post office	friend – acquaintance	phone – radio
TV – video recorder	pencil – ballpoint	letter – postcard
pullover – jacket	boots – shoes	wallet – purse

It's the most . . .

IN GROUPS OF 3 OR 4

This activity calls for a certain amount of imagination. If necessary, give examples to start the ball rolling:
> *An apple is the crispest one / sweetest one / easiest one to eat*
> *A grapefruit is the juiciest one / has the most pips / hardest one to eat (?)*
> *A pineapple is the most prickly one / prickliest one*
> *A lemon is the sourest one / most versatile one as an ingredient (?)*

It's much too big!

IN PAIRS

In case the writing load seems too heavy (8 × 4 = 32 sentences), get the pairs to just talk about each cartoon and afterwards only to write down sentences about the cartoons they found most stimulating. Allow time for them to compare their ideas with another group at the end.

In other words

These model answers are suggestions only:

Mexico is a warmer country than Canada.
It doesn't take as much skill to ride a bike as to drive a car.
He's the most arrogant person I know.
No one has ever said such a nice thing to me before.
It's too far for me to walk with my bad leg.
A DC-10 holds fewer passengers than a 747.
I think milk chocolate is nicer than plain chocolate.
This shirt isn't clean enough for me to wear.

19 REPORTED SPEECH: Statements

Summary

Practice in reporting statements made recently:
    He says that . . .   *He thinks that . . .*   *He believes that*
    He feels that . . .   *According to him . . .*   *Apparently . . .*
e.g. *He says that he's feeling sick.*

Reporting statements made some time ago:
    He said that . . .
    He told me that . . .   *He announced that . . .*   *He complained that . . .*
    He replied that . . .   *He answered that . . .*   *He explained that . . .*
    He added that . . .   *He admitted that . . .*   *He suggested that . . .*
e.g. *He said that he was feeling sick.*

Transforming verb forms when reporting conversations that took place in the past:
    'It's a long way.'   →   *He said that it was a long way.*
    'It'll be difficult.'   →   *He said that it would be difficult.*
    etc.

(*Practical English Usage* 533, 534)

Relevant errors

☆ He told me that he will do it yesterday.
☆ He said me that it was true.
☆ He told that it was true.
☆ She told me, that it was true.

What do you think?

AS A CLASS, THEN IN PAIRS

For this 'public opinion survey', students should be told to stand up and move around the classroom. If this is out of the question, students could just ask others who are within earshot. Form pairs at the outset: get one partner to start at the beginning of the list and the other to start at the end and work upwards.

The report-back-to-your-partner stage is the more important one, practising the use of different reporting verbs and requiring a report of the gist of everyone's opinions, not their exact words:

> *'One person I asked thinks that it's wrong to cheat in exams, but everyone else says that it's perfectly all right as long as you don't get caught.'*

Note that past verb forms *can* be used in such reports, if desired. However, as the opinions were expressed very recently, they can be considered as still 'present'.

What did he say?

AS A CLASS, THEN IN GROUPS OF 3

Make sure everyone studies the examples given and understands the grammatical points illustrated.

Point out that in some cases the actual times reported may have to be changed in the report itself. For example:

this week	may become	*that week*
today		*that day*
yesterday		*the day before*
next week		*the next week*
tomorrow		*the next day*
now		*then*
and *here*	may even become	*there*

The exercise itself should be done in writing, collaboratively in pairs, as it may look deceptively easy.

He admitted that he got frightened if there was a storm.

He complained that the sky was very cloudy that day.

He added that it would probably rain later.

He announced that he was going to take his new umbrella with him.

He explained that he had bought it the day before.

He suggested that he could use it for the first time.

He told me that he hadn't had a chance to try it out yet.

He told me that he wouldn't mind if it rained that day.

He added that he hoped there wouldn't be any thunder or lightning.

He told me that if he heard any thunder he'd stay indoors.

He admitted that he was a coward.

Clear up any problems at the end and reassure anyone who is unnerved by this exercise that in real life (though not in many exams) we report the gist of what has been said, in our own words, rather than every single word that was spoken.

➡→ Extra activity

AS A CLASS

Arrange the class in a large circle (or, if there's no room for this, in two or three smaller circles). The 'circle' needn't be round and could even be rectangular – just as long as it is continuous. The game requires everyone to report a series of statements from left to right round the circle until their own statement returns to them from the right. It might begin like this:
A (to B): I missed school last week because I had a cold.
B (to C): A said that he missed school last week because he had a cold.
C (to D): A said that he missed school last week when it was cold.
and so on.
At the end the original statement may have been somewhat distorted in the transmission.

This is a good opportunity to point out that the use of the past perfect in reported statements is often unnecessary, whatever the rule books say.

Guess what!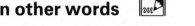

IN PAIRS

Student A should look at activity 34, while B looks at 51. Each student reports a conversation he or she has had with a female friend or with her husband. It turns out that the husband and wife have completely different recollections of their first meeting. Allow time at the end for everyone to comment on the activity and to ask any questions they wish to.

In other words 🖉

This transformation exercise can be done as homework or in class.

Annie told Bert that he ought to do something about his hair. He replied that he liked long hair and that it suited him. She answered that his hair looked ridiculous, though he disagreed with this. She pointed out that long hair like his hadn't been in

*fashion for years and he replied that he didn't care about fashion
and what mattered was whether he looked nice or not. She told
him that he looked awful in fact, particularly now that he was
going bald. Bert wouldn't accept this, but Annie suggested that
he was afraid to go to the hairdresser's in case they laughed. He
admitted that he hadn't been to the hairdresser's for a long time
and then Annie told him she had a good idea and offered to cut
his hair herself. When she suggested this and told him to sit
down he told her that he didn't trust her. He complained that she
might cut it so short that everyone would think he'd just come
out of the army.*

20 REPORTED SPEECH: Questions and requests

Summary

Practice in reporting *yes/no* questions and *Wh-* questions:
    He asked me if...   *He inquired if...*
    He wanted to know if...   *He asked me when...*
    He wondered if...   *He asked me where...*
    He tried to find out if...   *etc.*

Making word-order transformations in reported speech:
    'Is it true?'   →   *He wondered if it was true.*
    'When is it on?'   →   *He asked when it was on.*
    'What did you do?'   →   *He wanted to know what I did/had done.*

Reporting requests and other directives:
    She asked me to do it.
    She advised me to leave.
    She encouraged me to enter for the exam.

Using different reporting verbs appropriately:
    ask, order, want, persuade, invite, encourage, remind, etc.

(*Practical English Usage* 535, 536)

Relevant errors

☆ He asked me if I'll go there.
☆ She wanted to know when did I arrive.
☆ He asked me open the window.
☆ She advised me, 'Take the money'.
☆ He encouraged me doing it again.

What did he want to know?

IN PAIRS

This exercise is quite a hard one and may show students that reported speech in English can be quite tricky. For this reason, it is best done in writing – preferably collaboratively. Point out that *if* and *whether* are normally used

interchangeably and that to do the exercise they will need to use the
appropriate question words (*when, where, why,* etc.) in place of *if.*
Go through the right answers afterwards and answer any queries.

He wanted to know if I was all right.
He asked if I had had lunch.
He wondered if I wanted a drink.
He asked if I had managed to find my way easily.
He asked why I hadn't phoned them.
He tried to find out how long I was going to stay.
He asked if I would be seeing anyone else while I was there.
He wondered if I had met his mother, who was also staying
  there.
He asked if I minded sleeping on an airbed.
He asked me why I hadn't brought my sleeping bag.

➤➔ Extra activity

IN GROUPS OF 3

This light-hearted activity practises the use of reported speech to convey
messages and information to a third person.

Each group consists of A and C, who are *not on speaking terms,* and B who
conveys messages between them. The only way A and C can communicate is
through B, like this:
A: Ask him if he's all right.
B: She wants to know if you're all right.
C: Tell her that I'm fine.
B: He says he's fine. *or* He said that he was fine.
and so on.

The 'reports' can be made using present tenses or past tenses, though the
former sounds more natural in this context. Get each group to change roles
later so that everyone has a go at being the intermediary. Listen out for
word-order errors.

A very good day

ALONE FIRST, THEN IN PAIRS

1 Allow everyone some silent thinking time: 'Close your eyes and try to
  remember . . .'

2 Make sure the questioners really do ask for details and are using *direct* question forms accurately.
3 Instead of being done in writing (in class or as homework), this part could be done in rearranged pairs, where A + B and C + D become A + C and B + D. Then the reports can be given orally. Point out that the report itself should only contain the occasional reported question – not every single one that was asked.

What did she want you to do?

IN PAIRS

There are two parts to this exercise:
a) deciding on the functions, and
b) transforming the sentences.
If your class aren't up to the first part, it can be done as a class first. However, even the second part is quite tricky, so be ready to step in and offer help to any pairs who are making heavy weather of it.
    The answers shown below are suggestions only:

REQUEST	*She asked me to open the door.*
ADVICE	*She advised me to wear a raincoat.*
INVITATION	*She invited me to spend the weekend at their place.*
INVITATION	*She asked me to (go to) dinner with them.*
REMINDING	*She reminded me to bring a bottle of wine.*
RECOMMENDATION	*She recommended me to visit her country.*
ENCOURAGEMENT	*She encouraged me to enter the contest.*
WARNING	*She warned me not to go too near the edge of the lake.*
ORDER	*She ordered me to leave and not to come back.*
REQUEST	*She asked me to help her.*
ADVICE	*She advised me to learn the words by heart.*

In other words

IN GROUPS OF AT LEAST 4

The groups subdivide so that half the members look at activity 31 and the other half look at 48. They then work as sub-groups rewriting a reported conversation in dialogue form. It turns out that Dan's version of the conversation with Kate is quite different from her version of it.

When the sub-groups are ready, the groups re-form and they compare and discuss the two versions. (Many variations from the suggested versions below are possible.)

31

Dan: I'm seeing Lucy this evening.

Kate: What? You've just got to ring her up and break it all off.

Dan: Good grief, you've got a nerve. What right have you to try to tell me how to run my life?

Kate: Haha. Don't be so silly, Dan.

Dan: Look here, Kate, just get out of here and leave me alone.

Kate: No, don't take it like that. It's all for your own good. Let me explain . . .

Dan: I don't want to hear. Lucy is a very nice girl. Just go away and let me get on with my own life, all right?

Kate: If that's the way you want it, I'll go.

48

Kate: Oh, Dan, what are you planning to do? Do tell me.

Dan: I haven't a clue.

Kate: You've got to decide, you know.

Dan: Well, as I said, I just don't know what I'm going to do.

Kate: Well, you've got to make up your mind about Lucy pretty soon.

Dan: I suppose so, yes. What do you think I should do?

Kate: My advice is to ring her up and call the whole thing off. It's difficult, I know, but that's the only thing to do.

Dan: Oh dear, that's terrible! I can't live without her . . . but you're right I know. All right I will, but do please stay with me. I don't want to be alone.

Kate: I wish I could, but I've got a lot of things to do. Sorry. Goodbye.

Dan: Oh, Kate, do stay. Just for a few minutes. Please . . .

21 PREPOSITIONAL PHRASES I

Summary

Practice in using common prepositional phrases:
in bed, in pencil, in the rain and other phrases preceded by *in*
by heart, by accident, by mistake and other phrases preceded by *by*
on holiday, on purpose, on business and other phrases preceded by *on*
at home, at school, at work and other phrases preceded by *at*
out of date, out of sight, out of doors and other phrases preceded by
out of

Using prepositional phrases to describe means of travelling:
for a drive, for a walk, for a ride, etc.
on a journey, on an excursion, etc.
by car, by train, by bus, etc.
on a train, on a bus, on a plane, etc.
on the train, on the bus, on the plane, etc.
in a bus, in a train, in a plane, etc.
in the bus, in the train, in the plane, etc.

(*Practical English Usage* 486)

Relevant errors

☆ He is at bed.
☆ He said it at a loud voice.
☆ I went there by foot.
☆ I came by the train.
☆ I'm here on holiday.
☆ What happened on the end?
☆ She's out danger now.
☆ I travelled on plane.

IN

IN GROUPS OF 3

First of all, if necessary, go through the prepositional phrases shown and answer any questions. Then get each group to finish each sentence in *two* amusing or plausible ways. This can be done partially or wholly in writing. The answers given below are suggestions only:

Everyone laughed when he came to school *in his pyjamas.*

I'd rather be *in love* than *in pain.*

It's boring here indoors – let's go out *in the snow.*

I usually read the newspaper *in the evening.*

Poor Sam! He's got to spend three weeks *in hospital.*

She smiled sympathetically and then spoke to me *in a soft voice.*

He's having a bad time and he's often *in tears.*

You can see from her expression that she's *in a foul mood.*

Such an important meeting should be held *in public.*

In an exam it's best to write your answers *in ink.*

Going . . .

IN GROUPS OF 3 OR 4

Don't get bogged down in explaining the distinction between, for example:
   I came on the/a train   and   *I came in the/a train*   and   *I came by train*
– the difference is minimal in most cases and can't be tested in an exam either. The questions are designed to stimulate the members of a group to talk about many different ways of travelling. Add some questions of your own and find out from the class what they think are the best ways of getting to:
   some local towns, local beaches or swimming pools, local places of interest, different parts of the city and other countries near and far.

By heart

IN PAIRS

Begin by making sure everyone understands the phrases shown. The best ideas should be written down *later*, after the pairs have heard some other people's ideas, as this may produce some more memorable examples.

I've dialled 999 because *the building's on fire.*

We can't go to London today because *I'll be at school all day.*
The news must be true because *I heard it on the radio.*
I'm sure she's very clever because *she's at university now.*
I refuse to do any work at all because *I'm off duty.*
You can't punish them because *they didn't do it on purpose.*
They wouldn't let him enter the country because *his passport was out of date.*
Go away and don't be a nuisance and *leave me on my own.*
I'm not supposed to eat chocolate because *I'm on a diet.*
The only way to remember these phrases is *to learn them by heart.*

➨ Extra activity

AS A CLASS

To help everyone to remember the phrases that have come up in this unit, get the class to close their books and to shout out all the phrases they can remember. Like this:
Teacher:　　　　　　　AT . . .
Students (variously):　At home! At last! At the end! At a loss! etc.
Do the same with: IN, ON, FOR, BY and OUT OF.

Finally . . .

This exercise is essential if students are to remember the large number of phrases that have come up in this unit. However, it is up to them to decide which ones are the most difficult for them personally. If the exercise is to be done as homework, perhaps the deciding-which-ones part should be done in class first.

22 PREPOSITIONAL PHRASES II

Summary

Practice in using prepositional phrases that include the word *time*:
  on time, in time, before my time, behind the times, etc.

Using common preposition + noun + preposition phrases:
  in addition to, with the help of, in the mood for, etc.

Using prepositional phrases that operate as 'discourse markers':
  on the one hand . . . on the other hand, in fact, in general, etc.

(For complete lists see the Student's Book.)
(*Practical English Usage* 172, 606, 486)

Relevant errors

☆ He arrived on the nick of time.   ☆ That's right in the theory.
☆ In answer of your question . . .   ☆ He's in charge the office.
☆ I'm in mood for some music.   ☆ He never arrives at time.

Time flies!

IN PAIRS

Get everyone to look through the phrases shown and ask any questions they
wish to (*on time* = punctually, *in time* = not too late, etc.). Perhaps point out
that *It's about time* + past can be avoided by saying *It's about time to*
+ infinitive.

   After doing the exercise, preferably in writing, the pairs should hear some
other students' ideas.

If you go by plane *be sure to arrive in good time.*
The twins *always answer at the same time.*
The lifeboat *got to the ship in the nick of time.*
Everyone ought to *be able to relax from time to time.*
Poor old Grandma, she's *behind the times.*
After all this bad weather *it's about time we had some sunshine.*

At the end of the exam *I found I was out of time.*
If you're going to an interview, *make sure you arrive on time.*

---

in time for . . .

IN PAIRS

Get everyone to look through the phrases and ask questions first. Then get them to do the exercise collaboratively, preferably in writing. Go through the exercise as a class afterwards.

I know it's late but am I still *in time for* dinner?
The assistant manager signed the report *on behalf of* Mr Brown.
Mr Brown is the person who is *in charge of* this department.
My sister says that she's *in love with* her maths teacher!
We're having a big party *in honour of* Mum and Dad's golden wedding.
I was *on the point of leaving* when you arrived.
The audience started clapping and cheering *at the end of* the show.
I could see a figure hiding in the cellar *by the light of* my torch.
They're playing Beatles records on the radio *in memory of* John Lennon.
I think I'll go out for a walk because I'm not *in the mood for* studying.
The magician lifted the table *with the help of* his two assistants.
The two countries are still *at war with* each other after all this time.
In answer to your question, wait and see!
They went up the Amazon in 1925 *in search of* Eldorado.

On the one hand . . .

IN PAIRS

This exercise gives a foretaste of unit 37 on joining sentences. After getting the pairs to do it collaboratively in writing, go through it with the whole class.

There are two ways of looking at this issue: *on the one hand* our profits will probably rise, but *on the other hand* we'll have to make some sacrifices.
I'm going to have to take $500 as pocket money, *at any rate* that's what I was told.
Jack has some strange ideas: *according to him,* women are inferior to men! ⟫→

I see what you mean and *in theory* I agree with you but I don't think your
ideas will work *in practice.*

There are a number of changes to be made: *for instance,* staff must arrive
on time in the morning.

He isn't the best of my students: *as a matter of fact* he ought to work much
harder.

I know it's not a pleasant thing to have to do, but I'm sure that *on the whole*
you won't regret doing it.

▶→ Extra activity

AS A CLASS

Pick out from this unit and unit 21 at least 20 prepositional phrases that your
students have found tricky. Say the beginning of a sentence that might call for
the use of each phrase and get members of the class to shout out ways of
completing it. These sentences can be invented by yourself or taken from the
exercises themselves. For example:

Teacher: The fire brigade arrived . . .
Students: . . . in the nick of time.
        . . . because the house was on fire.
        . . . after I'd called them on the phone.
        etc.

A little walk

Make it clear that this exercise calls for the use of both single-word
prepositions and prepositional phrases from both unit 21 and 22. It can be
done in class or as homework.

The weather was so nice *in* the afternoon that I decided to go *for* a little walk
in my new boots – the ones I'd seen advertised *on* TV as 'the world's best
boots'. Well, *in* theory, yes, they were very comfortable boots but I soon
found that *in* fact they gave me blisters. Now, *in general* I do enjoy walking
but by now I was *in* such a lot of pain that I was *in* a very bad mood. All I
wanted was rest and refreshment, *in other words* I needed to sit down,
have a drink and go home *on* the bus. The last bus home was in half an hour
from the nearest village so I would have to get there *in* a hurry. *At* last I got
to the village *just in* time for a drink at the pub before the bus came. I limped
to the bus stop *in* the hope *of* getting on, but I was *out of* luck because the

bus was full up – not even standing room! I knew I'd never make it home *on* foot and I was *on* the point *of* returning to the pub to drown my sorrows when another bus came round the corner, completely empty. I got on, bought my ticket, sat *by myself* at the back and started to feel *at* peace *with* the world again as I took off my boots!

23 ARTICLES: *a, the* or *Ø*?

Summary

Practice in using *a, an, the* or *Ø (zero article) appropriately:*
I like apples	(in general)
I'd like an apple.	(one, please)
I didn't like the apple.	(that particular one)
I didn't like the apples.	(those particular ones)
The work I do can be dull.	(not all work, just mine)

Using articles accurately to talk about occupations and subjects:
He's a doctor.
Doctors are wonderful.
He's studying medicine.
Archaeology is fascinating.

Using *the* or *Ø* accurately in common phrases:
the country, the seaside, the USA, the UK, the police, etc.
North America, music, jazz, classical music, Cambridge University,
   loneliness, rudeness, anger, shame, etc.
in (the) town, on (the) TV, etc.
out of the window, on the bus, on the phone, in the newspaper, etc.
for lunch, in bed, to school, at school, by car, etc.
all the people, most of the time, the one I like, etc.

(*Practical English Usage* 71, 65, 66, 67, 68, 69, 70)

Relevant errors

☆ I like the apples in general.
☆ He's going to be doctor.
☆ I'm studying the linguistics.
☆ The doctors are wonderful.
☆ I finished all work.
☆ You'd better go to the bed.
☆ I came here by the car.
☆ I need a aspirin.
☆ Send for a police.
☆ I love the classical music.

Apples

IN PAIRS

Begin by getting everyone to fill in the gaps in the conversation with *a, an, the, some* or *0* (*0* means 'nothing' or 'zero article').

Lady: Would you like *an* apple?
Guest: Ooh, yes please! I love *0* apples.
Lady: Well, there's *a* big one and *some* small ones.
Guest: Oh, I'll have *a* small one please.
Lady: Are you sure you won't have *the* big one?
Guest: Yes thanks. Mmm! What *a* tasty apple!
Lady: Good. And I'll have *the* big one myself.

1 This part of the exercise can be done quickly or cut short if your students find it too easy. Alternatively, do it as a class so that you can gauge when to stop and go on to part 2.
2 If necessary, write up on the board some of these useful adjectives that can be used:
    nice, delicious, tasty, juicy, refreshing, mouth-watering, yummy . . .
    nasty, awful, dreadful, appalling, repulsive, disgusting, sour,
        nauseating . . .

▶→ Extra activity

AS A CLASS

Get everyone to look around them at the room they're in – and if possible out of the window and out of the door too. Then get each member of the class to think of one thing or a group of things they have seen. The others have to play 'I Spy' and guess what is in the first player's mind. The only clue they have is the first letter of the word. Like this:
First player: T for tango.
Other students: One of the tables? A pair of trousers? The top of a pen? One of the trees outside?
First player: Yes, but which one?
Other student: The one on the right?
First player: That's right, your turn.
and so on.

What a job!

IN PAIRS

1 Again, if this seems too easy, don't leave it out but do it quickly or cut it short – you never know what errors might be made otherwise.
2 Encourage students to suggest a *variety* of possible careers: for example, Geoff might become a translator, an interpreter, a sales representative, a lecturer, etc.

In bed

IN PAIRS

Get the pairs to *answer* the questions as well as filling in gaps (or leaving them blank). Alternatively, get everyone to answer the questions at the end as a class.

If you've got a cold, do you go to Ø bed or go to Ø work as usual?

Do you buy your clothes at *a* local shop or in *(the)* town?

If you wanted to learn Russian, would you go to *(a)* school or use *a* dictionary?

Do you usually eat a lot for Ø lunch or do you just have *a* snack?

When you look out of *the* window in *the* room you're in now, what can you see?

What kind of Ø music do you like: Ø jazz, Ø rock or Ø classical music?

Do you know someone who has been to *the* Unites States, Ø North Africa or *the* Soviet Union?

Do you come to Ø school by Ø car, on Ø foot or on *the* bus?

Spot the errors

IN PAIRS

Make sure all the errors are accurately pinpointed and then corrected.

```
                       the
I love X mountains and I adore x seaside too.
        a                      an
I've got the headache and I need x aspirin.
                         the                      the
I don't like talking on a telephone, I prefer to write the letters.
       a                                           a
He's the very good friend of mine even though he has the bad temper.
                                                    a
He's studying the music because he wants to become/famous musician.
                                                 the
I'm going to watch X TV tonight to see a film about the Cambridge University.
         the
I read in/newspaper that we're going to have X fine weather.
      the                                        the
When X police arrived, they questioned all/people in the building.
```

A writer's life

This (only *partly* autobiographical) story can be done as homework or collaboratively in pairs.

As *a* writer, I seem to spend *0* most of *the* time working at *0* home in *the* office, sitting in *0* front of *the* typewriter. In fact, *the* only people I see regularly are *the* members of my family and it is difficult to keep in *0* touch with *the* friends I made at *0* school. I'm always getting *0* letters and *0* phone calls from *the* people at *the* publisher's, though, and I do try to go out of *the* house at least once *a* day. And from *0* time to time I give *0* lectures or take part in *0* courses at *0* conferences or at *0* schools in *the* UK or *0* abroad and this helps to prevent me feeling too isolated. I also get *0* reports back from *the* schools where *the* material I've written is being tried out, and this kind of *0* feedback is very useful. Still, it seems to me that while I'm still busy and continue to make *a* living, I should go on writing *0* books. But as soon as *the* ideas seem to be drying up or I start suffering from *0* loneliness, I'll give up *0* writing and get back into *a* classroom and meet *some* students again.

24 *If* SENTENCES: Types 1 and 2

Summary

Practice in using *if, unless, when* and *till/until** in sentences like:
I can't do it unless you help me.
I can't do it if you don't help me.
I'll be able to do it when you agree to help me.

Recognising the difference in meaning between sentences using *if* + present, *if* + past and *if* + past perfect:
If I see him I'll tell him. (I may see him) – 'Type 1' conditional
If I saw him I'd tell him. (but I can't or won't see him) – 'Type 2' conditional
If I had seen him I'd have told him. (but I didn't see him) – 'Type 3' conditional

Using *if* or *unless* + present (Type 1 conditional) appropriately:
If I wake up early I'll go for a run.
If I don't wake up early I won't go for a run.
I won't go for a run unless I wake up early.

Using *if* + past (Type 2 conditional) appropriately:
If I knew more I'd/I would pass the exam.
If I knew more I might/could pass the exam.
If I was/were cleverer I'd/I would pass.*

*Students can regard these as interchangeable.

(*Practical English Usage* 303, 304, 306)

Relevant errors

☆ I'll buy it unless I have enough money.
☆ If I would be rich I would be happy.
☆ If I am rich I'll buy a yacht tomorrow.
☆ If I'd be rich I'll buy a Porsche.
☆ Life would be easier when I were rich.
☆ If I'll see him I'll tell him.
☆ If I saw him I'd told him.

If and *unless*

IN PAIRS

This exercise introduces the differences in use between the conjunctions *if*, *unless*, *when* and *till/until* (which are interchangeable). Go through the exercise after the pairs have finished, making sure everyone is aware of the variations possible.

It won't work *unless/until* you put batteries in.
Come and see me *if* you feel lonely.
Don't phone me *unless* you need my help.
You can't do it *unless* you have permission.
Let's wait *until* our friends arrive.
Let's have coffee *when/if* we've finished.
We'll drive *unless* you want to walk.
I can't work *if/when* you keep interrupting.

What are you going to do?

IN PAIRS

This 'pattern conversation' allows students to use *if* and *unless* in a controlled piece of practice. Encourage the more adventurous students to depart from the pattern once they have mastered the grammatical forms.

Afterwards, get the pairs to ask each other what their *real* plans are for the next few days and to say what each plan depends on.

If, if, if . . .

IN GROUPS OF 3

This exercise shows the difference between the three types of conditional sentences. Encourage the groups to produce several ideas for the last sentence.

If you drive carefully, you *won't* have any accidents.
If I *was/were* a better driver, I *wouldn't* have so many accidents.
If I *had driven* carefully last night, I *wouldn't have had* an accident.
If I *was/were* President of the United States, I*'d re-start disarmament talks.*

101

Just suppose . . .

IN GROUPS OF 3

DANGER: If a member of your class is embarrassingly tall, short, unintelligent, ugly, old, etc., this activity may need careful handling. Make it clear that this is supposed to be light-hearted and that statements like:

If I were much taller, people wouldn't despise me so much.

are *not* called for. Instead sentences like the following are preferable:

If I were taller I'd be able to touch the ceiling.
If I were much more intelligent I could become a university professor.
If I was much more patient I wouldn't get angry when I have to queue.
    etc.

If this activity fails to provoke some students, get them to *write* one sentence about each idea. Perhaps also suggest how much older or younger and how much taller or shorter they may imagine themselves to be: 'five years younger', '50 cm taller', etc.

First prize!

IN GROUPS OF 3

Make sure each group discusses its reasons for its choices. Perhaps get them to persuade each other that what they would choose is the best for the whole group:

'It'd be best to take the villa because then we'd be able to spend our holidays there – we could take it in turns. The rest of the year we could rent it out.'

➡ Extra activity

IN GROUPS OF 3 OR 4

In this activity the members of each group decide how they would spend the 'perfect weekend' together, assuming of course they had plenty of money to spend. Where would they go? What would they do?

Ask each group to explain its fantasy to the rest of the class at the end.

Complete the sentences

This exercise can be done collaboratively in class or as homework. The answers below are suggestions only:

If I get up late tomorrow, *I'll miss school.*
If it snows a lot this winter, *we can go skiing.*
If I lived in the USA, *I'd miss my family.*
If I have a headache tomorrow, *I'll stay in bed.*
If I were a nicer person, *everyone would like me.*
Unless you leave immediately, *I'll call the police.*
I won't come and see you if *you don't invite me.*
I wouldn't be very happy if *I came last in the race.*
The world would be a better place if *there was no hunger.*
I'm not going out tonight unless *I get bored.*
I would speak perfect English if *I was British.*
I'll take a message if *you can't phone back.*

25 *If* SENTENCES: Type 3

Summary

Practice in using Type 3 conditionals:
If I'd known I'd have told her.
If I had known I would have told her.
If she hadn't seen him, she wouldn't have found out.
If she had seen him, she might/could have felt upset.

Using 'mixed' Type 2/3 conditionals appropriately:
If I had been born 100 years ago, I wouldn't be alive today.
I wouldn't have made that mistake if I was clever.

Using Types 1, 2 and 3 conditionals appropriately:
If the weather's nice, we'll go out later.
If I had lots of money, I'd give it all away.
If I'd known the price, I wouldn't have tried it on.

(*Practical English Usage* 303, 304)

Relevant errors

☆ If I would have known, I wouldn't have told him.
☆ If I had known I hadn't told him.
☆ If I had been born 100 years ago, I wouldn't have been here now.
☆ If I was born 100 years ago, I would be very old now.

She didn't win

IN PAIRS OR ALONE

To start things off, perhaps get the class to suggest what kind of opportunities are open to the lucky (?) winner of such a contest.

Afterwards see if anyone has any strong feelings about beauty contests and all that they imply. What qualities would be required of a *Mr* World winner? Strength? Being 18 years old? Intelligence? Charm? Nice legs?

➤→ **Extra activity**

IN PAIRS

This straightforward activity will help to build confidence in using Type 3 conditionals. Each student pretends to admire his or her partner's clothes and possessions, like this:

A: That's a nice bag!

B: Do you like it? It was only £12.99. If it'd been much more expensive, I wouldn't have bought it. By the way, I like your shoes.

A: Oh, do you? They were very expensive actually. In fact, if I hadn't had some money to spend for my birthday, I wouldn't have been able to afford them.

and so on.

The conversations can include books, watches, pens and bicycles as well as visible clothing.

If I'd been there . . .

IN PAIRS

Less imaginative pairs could be asked to choose just six of the places and write a sentence about each. Each sentence should follow the pattern:

If I'd been in (place) *in* (year) . . .

Luckily . . .

IN GROUPS OF 3

Encourage each member of the group to suggest a different ending for each of the sentences. The answers below are suggestions only:

Luckily my brakes worked all right, but if they hadn't worked, I might have crashed.

Luckily I soon got better, but if I hadn't got better, I might still be in hospital.

Luckily I only got a black eye, but if I had been hit harder, I might have got a broken nose.

Luckily I got the job easily enough, but if I had been less well-qualified, I wouldn't have got the job.

Luckily the rain stopped after breakfast, but if it had gone on raining, we wouldn't have been able to go out.   ⟫→

Luckily I got to the cinema early enough, but if I had been delayed, I'd have missed the beginning of the film.
Luckily our pilot managed to land the plane on one engine, but if he hadn't been so skilful, we might have all been killed.

Just imagine . . . !

IN GROUPS OF 3 OR 4

1　This part is best done in a single-sex group: all males or all females in each of the groups. Then everyone can feel free to use their imaginations without embarrassment. Perhaps get the groups to list five nice aspects of a sex-change and five unpleasant ones. Afterwards the lists can be discussed in rearranged mixed-sex groups or pairs.
2　At the end of part 2, get each group to suggest its most amusing or thought-provoking ideas.

In other words

IN PAIRS OR ALONE

Point out that *if* should be used in every sentence and that some of the sentences require the use of mixed conditionals.

We stayed up all night and that's why we're all so tired this morning.
We *wouldn't all be so tired this morning if we hadn't stayed up all night.*

She wasn't able to answer the questions and so she failed the exam.
If she *had been able to answer the questions, she wouldn't have failed the exam.*

I didn't see you there, otherwise I'd have said hallo.
If I *had seen you there, I'd have said hallo.*

The reason why I haven't been to America is that I can't afford it.
If I *had (had) enough money I would have been to America.*

He hasn't studied English before and that's why he's in a beginners class.
If he *had studied English before, he wouldn't be in a beginners class.*

They didn't go to the seaside because the weather was so bad.

They *would have gone to the seaside if the weather had been better.*

One of the reasons why I didn't phone you was that I was very busy.

I might *have phoned you if I hadn't been so busy.*

They won the match because two of our players were injured.

If *two of our players had been fit, we wouldn't have lost the match.*

Three paragraphs

This written work consolidates what has been practised in this unit and unit 24.

26 RELATIVE CLAUSES

Summary

Practice in using *who*, *that*, *which*, *where* and *whose* in 'identifying relative clauses':
> *This is the man (who/that) I told you about.*
> *This is the man who/that told me about it.*
> *That was the film (which/that) I saw yesterday.*
> *That was the film which/that won the Oscar.*
> *That is the woman whose husband has left her.*
> *The university where he teaches is Exeter.*

Omitting *who*, *that* or *which* as the object of the relative clause:
> *He is the man I told you about.*
> *Those are the books I mentioned.*

Using *who*, *which*, *where*, *when* and *whose* in 'non-identifying relative clauses':
> *My (only) son, who is three years old, is very mischievous.*
> *My house, where I have lived for seven years, is on a main road.*
> *My house, which cost £13,000 when we bought it, is now worth much more.*
> *Tuesday, when she has her piano lesson, is her favourite day.*
> *My best friend, whose name is Tim, lives in the North.*

Using *who* and *which* to connect sentences (as conjunctions):
> *I enjoy the work of Robert Redford, who starred in The Candidate.*
> *The Candidate, which was directed by Michael Ritchie, is a fine film.*
> *She was very shy and blushed, which I found charming.*

(*Practical English Usage* 525, 526, 527, 528, 530)

Relevant errors

☆ The girl which is in my class wears glasses.
☆ The girl, who is wearing glasses, is my sister.
☆ His mother who lives alone has grey hair.
☆ I saw Peter who waved at me.
☆ Everything what I said was true.
☆ My car, that is in the garage, is out of action.

This is the man who . . .

AS A CLASS

The illustration shows that *who* can be omitted if it's the object of the relative clause. (Point out that *who* and *that* are interchangeable here.) Get the class to suggest continuations to the conversation beginning: *'That's the man . . .'*

➡→ Extra activity

AS A CLASS

To develop fluency in using identifying relative clauses, use a set of magazine pictures or ads. Distribute them among the class and get everyone to comment on the pictures or ads like this:
   'This is the one (that/which) I like best because . . .'
   'That's the one that/which appeals to me most because . . .'
   'Which is the one that/which seems the best to you?'
Each comment must include *the one, the man, the picture* or *the advertisement*.

What's she called?

IN PAIRS

Student A looks at activity 35. Student B looks at activity 44. Student A can easily work out some of the girls' names but can't recognise the others. Student B has complementary information. Following the pattern given, they exchange information and manage to identify all the girls and say what they know about them all. Perhaps give another example first:
B: What's the name of the girl with the curly hair / who has curly hair?
A: She's called Belinda.
B: Oh really? She's the girl who was in my class at school.

What's it about?

IN GROUPS OF 3

Student A looks at activity 37, B looks at 43 and C looks at 56. Each has information about some of the works listed. The others have to find out about the other works by asking questions like:
   'What's Superman about?' and getting the answer:
   'Superman's about a man who can fly and has other super-human powers.'

My friend John, whose . . . 　📝

IN PAIRS

Before the pairs do this exercise collaboratively, make sure they are quite clear on the difference between 'identifying' and 'non-identifying' relative clauses (also known as 'defining' or 'non-defining' relatives). Point out the different punctuation and different stress and intonation when saying, for example:

My friend who's abroad is having a holiday.
My mother, who's abroad, is having a holiday.

Edinburgh , *where I went to* college, is a beautiful city.
My eldest brother , *who has a* moustache , is studying architecture.
The man *that appeared on* television is a famous writer.
The day *when I got* married was Friday the 13th.
On Wednesday , *when I went to the* cinema , it rained all day.
The car *which was* stolen was a yellow Rolls Royce.
My car , *which was made in* 1965 , is a yellow Morris 1000.
Liverpool , *who are top of the* First Division, have an unbeatable team.
But the team *which won the* Cup Final are in the Second Division.

Connections

IN PAIRS

This exercise is best done in writing. It practises the use of relative pronouns as conjunctions to form complex sentences.

Mary ate four cream cakes, which made her feel sick.
I'm going on holiday to the mountains, which I'm really looking forward to.
I went to see a film about space monsters, which gave me nightmares.
We started talking to Bernard, who told us about his adventures in the jungle.
I wrote them an angry letter, which made me feel much calmer (afterwards).
I spent a long time with James, who was very helpful and gave me some good advice.
You'd better rewrite this letter, which you wrote far too quickly and carelessly.

In other words

The answers below are suggestions only.

The clothes he was wearing were old and dirty.
The day I started work was January 2.
The person who gave me the message was wearing a yellow pullover.
Some Like it Hot, *which was made in 1959, is my favourite film.*
The girl who gave me a kiss is an old school friend of mine.
The lady whose husband you were rude to is upset now.
The shoes I bought were in the sale.
Green, which reminds me of the countryside, is the colour I love.

27 ADJECTIVES AND VERBS + PREPOSITION I

Summary

This is the first of two units on verbs and adjectives with prepositions. Further idiomatic prepositional verbs are practised in unit 38.

Practice in using adjectives + *at* to talk about proficiency:
  good at, bad at, brilliant at, hopeless at, etc.
e.g. *She's hopeless at tennis but brilliant at darts.*

Using adjectives/participles + *about* or + *of* to describe feelings:
  angry about, annoyed about, glad about, nervous about, etc.
  afraid of, frightened of, scared of, terrified of, etc.
e.g. *I'm worried about the written exam and scared of the oral part.*

Using the correct preposition after certain common adjectives:
  ashamed of, unkind to, polite to, proud of, different to/from,
  responsible for, impressed by/with, jealous of, sorry for/about,
  friendly to, rude to, etc.
e.g. *It's horrid to be unkind to animals.*

Using the correct preposition after certain common verbs:
  praise someone for, remind someone of, congratulate someone on,
  forgive someone for, blame someone for, name someone after,
    punish someone for, etc.
  take part in, crash into, prepare for, belong to, depend on, concentrate on,
  consist of, complain about, succeed in, divide into, pay for, etc.
e.g. *She reminds me of someone I once knew.*
    We crashed into the car in front.

(*Practical English Usage* 485)

Relevant errors

☆ He's good in football.
☆ He was glad for winning the match.
☆ I'm ashamed by my behaviour.
☆ We succeeded on winning.

☆ I congratulated him for his success.
☆ This depends of what you mean.

Any good at maths?

IN PAIRS

Encourage each pair to use a variety of adjectives, not just *good* and *bad*. The activity can be speeded up by omitting part 2.

How do you feel?

IN PAIRS AND AS A CLASS

After the pairs have fitted the adjectives and prepositions into the appropriate gaps, get the class to admit to the kinds of things they:
   are frightened of, get angry about, get nervous about, feel happy about, etc.

The numbers show which words might fit in each situation:

She's *1*.
getting the job.

He's *2*.
tomorrow's exam.

She's *3*.
going out alone at night.

He's *4*.
being kept waiting.

She's *5*.
missing the show.

He's *6*.
leaving his girlfriend.

4 angry	*6 heart-broken*	*1 glad*
4 annoyed	*2,3 worried*	*2 nervous*
1 delighted	*5,6 upset*	*1 pleased*
5 disappointed	*6 depressed*	*1 thrilled*
1 happy	*4 furious*	*2 anxious*
		5,6 sad

+ about

3 afraid
3 scared
3 terrified
3 frightened

+ of

Add the prepositions

IN PAIRS

If the class have no idea what prepositions are missing, run through the adjectives in the exercise quickly supplying the missing prepositions *only*. Don't let anyone write them in at this stage, though.

Miss Green's a very nice lady and tries to be friendly *to everybody she meets*.

Pete's the sort of nasty person who is unkind *to children and animals*.

I always try to be as polite as possible *to the people I deal with*.

When Tom got promotion he was very proud *of his large new office*.

Life in my country is quite different *from/to life in the* UK.

The insurance company wants to know who was responsible *for the accident*.

Foreigners who visit my country are always impressed *by/with the friendliness of the people*.

When Mary started tennis lessons, John became very jealous *of the tennis coach*.

The little boy said he was very sorry *for/about what he had done*.

When Vera introduced Neil to her family, he was very rude *to her father and mother*.

Rearrange the sentences

IN PAIRS

Unlikely combinations may be amusing, but may also mess up the other sentences!

Everyone praised him *for*   his own stupidity.
This house reminds me *of*   Winston Churchill.
We congratulated him *on*   telling lies and cheating in the exam.
I can't forgive him *for*   doing so well in the exam.
He tried to blame us *for*   his performance in the concert.
They named their son *after*   a place I used to know.
He punished his son *for*   speaking to me in such an insulting way.

Verbs + prepositions

IN PAIRS

This exercise should be done in class if possible. Again it may be necessary to run quickly through the missing prepositions beforehand.

I broke her glasses and she made me pay *for having them repaired.*

He wasn't paying attention and crashed *into a stationary car.*

I've got to stay at home tonight and prepare *for my lessons tomorrow.*

All the furniture in this room belongs *to my landlord.*

Whether or not we go out depends *on the weather.*

There was so much noise that I couldn't concentrate *on what I was trying to do.*

The United Kingdom consists *of England, Scotland, Wales and Northern Ireland.*

It was an awful hotel and we complained *about the poor service and the dirty room.*

She made a tremendous effort and succeeded *in winning the race.*

We only had one cake, so it was divided *between us / into four pieces.*

➤→ Extra activity

AS A CLASS

Pick out the adjectives and verbs that caused any problems in this unit. Call out the words one by one and ask the class to shout out the missing preposition. Like this:

Teacher: Consist...
Class: Consist of!
Teacher: Anxious...
Class: Anxious about!
and so on.

28 ADJECTIVES AND VERBS + PREPOSITION II

Summary

Practice in using verbs that are followed by an indirect object or a preposition + object:

give, sell, lend, bring, offer, return, deliver, give back, take, buy, get, steal, receive, borrow

e.g. *He gave me the book.*
He gave the book to me.
I got the book from him.

Using prepositions after certain common verbs:

look for, search for, look after, look at, stare at, throw something to, throw something at, open fire on, shoot at, shout at, laugh at, laugh about, pay attention to, take notice of, care about, care for, take care of, have a word with someone about, speak to someone about, disagree with someone about, talk to someone about, argue with someone about, have a nightmare about, dream about, dream of, think of, think about, could do with, can't do without, call for, call someone after

e.g. *I'm looking for my pen.*
Please look after my cat.

(*Practical English Usage* 485)

Relevant errors

☆ I got from him the book.
☆ I'm looking after my lost wallet.
☆ Look after me when I'm talking to you.
☆ Please don't laugh to me.
☆ Can you look for my cats when I'm on holiday?
☆ He gave to me the book.

Who to? Where from?

Uninspired pairs may need some prompting with topics to talk about. Here
are some suggestions (which can be written up on the board):
PEOPLE: robber, policeman, detective, sales assistant, my best friend, bus
           driver, barman, etc.
OBJECTS: borrowed money, rented car, library books, stolen jewels, new
           furniture, a round of drinks, etc.
Note that *get* and *buy* can also be followed by *for* or an indirect object:
    I'll get it for you.   *I'll get you it.*
    I'll buy you one.   *I'll buy one for you.*

Add the prepositions

The verbs beside each of the cartoons are loosely grouped together for ease
of understanding and memorising. When the pairs have finished the exercise,
get them to test each other: one of them closes the book, while the other reads
aloud the beginning of each sentence and gets his or her partner to supply the
missing prepositions. Like this:
A: I've looked everywhere . . .
B: Um . . . for my keys.
A: Right. He threw the ball . . .
They can take turns in doing this with each group of sentences.

I've looked everywhere *for* my keys.
We searched high and low *for* them.
Who's going to look *after* the children while you're away?
He tends to feel embarrassed when people look *at* him.
Don't you know it's rude to stare *at* people?

He threw the ball *to* his friend who caught it easily.
The rioters started throwing stones *at* the police.
The police opened fire *on* the crowd.
They went on shooting *at* them until they ran away.
She gets very upset if someone shouts *at* her.
Don't laugh *at* him or he'll get very angry.
Afterwards they were able to laugh *about* the incident.

Take no notice *of* him, he's just showing off.
Please pay attention *to* what I tell you.
He's very tactless and doesn't care *about* other people.
None for me, thanks, I don't really care *for* chocolate.
Who's going to take care *of* me if I feel ill?

I'd like a word *with* you *about* your work.
He spoke *to* me *about* his plans.
I disagreed *with* him *about* what he should do.
She talked *to* him *about* the book she'd read.
He argued *with* her *about* the opinion she'd expressed.

I had a nightmare *about* prehistoric monsters.
I was dreaming *about* my childhood before I woke up.
I'm dreaming *of* going to Africa one day.
She's thinking *of* changing her job.
I was just thinking *about* how to solve the problem.

I could do *with* a nice cool drink.
I can't do *without* eight hours sleep a night.
I'll call *for* you at 7.30 in my car.
They called him Michael *after* his grandfather.
We called *for* the bill after our meal.

(Unit 38 follows up this exercise with some more idiomatic prepositional verbs.)

➤→ **Extra activity**

AS A CLASS

To help everyone to remember what has been practised in this and the previous unit, and to encourage the use of the expressions in sentences, this memory game is useful.

Divide the class into two teams and get members of each team to supply a sentence using the words you challenge them with. For example:

Teacher: Team A. Your word is *complain.*
Member of Team A: They complained about the service in the restaurant.
Teacher: Good, 1 point. Team B: *laugh.*
Member of Team B: Everyone laughed at him.
and so on.
(If no member of a team can produce a correct sentence, a bonus point can be
awarded to the other team if they can do it.)

Do you remember?

This exercise requires students to remember and use verbs or adjectives +
prepositions from units 27 and 28:

It's all my fault – can you ever *forgive me for* what I've done?

Getting the job *depends on* how well you do at the interview.

Congratulations on passing your exams!

I'd like to *speak to* the manager about this, please.

When I finish my studies, I'm *thinking of* travelling round the world.

I usually feel *nervous about* going anywhere by plane.

Don't be silly! There's no need to be *afraid of* flying!

I'm ever so hungry – I *could do with* a sandwich or something.

I used to be *awful at* spelling but now I'm a bit better.

All right, then! Which one of you *is responsible for* breaking the window?

It's your own fault! Don't *blame me for* your own mistakes!

Tom's grandmother *looked after him* when his parents died.

That's a nice watch, where did you *get it from*?

Shh! I'm trying to *concentrate on* my homework.

She looks very *happy about* something – she's actually smiling!

29 THE PASSIVE

Summary

Practice in using the passive in various different grammatical forms:
He isn't liked.
He is being watched.
He was being followed.
He was shot.
He has been dismissed.
He had been given his notice.
Being told you're stupid is unpleasant.
I dislike being laughed at.

Using the passive when describing actions where the agent is unknown or unimportant:
He has been murdered.
I don't like being criticised.
He was jailed for three months.

Using the passive when placing 'known information' at the beginning and 'new information' at the end of a sentence:
Some of Shakespeare's plays may have been written by Bacon.
The book I was telling you about was written by Paul Scott.

Transforming active sentences to the passive and vice versa:
The judge sent him to prison.   →   *He was sent to prison.*
He was punished by his father.   →   *His father punished him.*

(*Practical English Usage* 457, 458, 459, 460, 267)

Relevant errors

☆ My watch is been stolen.
☆ Macbeth was written from Shakespeare.
☆ The victim killed at midnight.
☆ This has written by someone else.

In other words

IN PAIRS

This exercise introduces the use of the passive in different forms.
Check each pair's work for accuracy. Any theories on who was the
murderer?

The body was found in the study.
The murder was committed at around midnight.
Two strangers were seen near the house (by the butler).
The butler is being questioned (by the police).
Lady Wessex is known to have been out of the country.
The younger son has not been seen for three weeks.
The elder son was last seen two years ago.
Lord Wessex will be sadly missed.

Who by?

IN GROUPS OF 3

If necessary, begin by getting members of the class to tell the less well-
informed students that Guernica is a painting, Star Wars is a film, The Magic
Flute an opera and so on. Preferably, however, let the groups sort this out for
themselves by process of elimination as they do the activity. After they've
done the easy ones (Mickey Mouse, Snoopy, etc.), the more esoteric ones will
fall into place. Nonetheless, be prepared to offer groups some clues if they get
stuck.

   Make sure this activity is done orally or in writing (not just by drawing
connecting lines!) and that appropriate verbs are used:

Nicholas Nickleby was written by Charles Dickens.
Guernica was painted by Picasso.
The Magic Flute was composed by Mozart.
Star Wars was directed by George Lucas.
The 'Unfinished' Symphony was left incomplete by Schubert.
Snoopy is drawn by Charles Schulz.
*Sergeant Pepper's Lonely Hearts Club Band was made by the
   Beatles.*
Penicillin was discovered by Alexander Fleming.
Light bulbs were invented by Thomas Edison.
Walkman stereo is manufactured by Sony.

War and Peace was written by Leo Tolstoy.
Mickey Mouse was invented by Walt Disney.
This book is published by Cambridge University Press.

News headlines

IN PAIRS

Each headline should become a passive sentence, though some might be rewritten in other ways too.

Over 100 people were killed on the roads last month.
24,000 people were murdered in the USA last year.
An ancient statue has been found in a garden shed.
15 students have been arrested after a demonstration.
Teachers will be given a pay rise this year.
A bank manager is still being held by the police.
Mr Jones has been made a Cabinet Minister.
The divorce law will not be changed till 1994.
15 new hospitals were built last year.
The tennis championship has been won by a British girl (or man?).

Being ...

IN PAIRS

Student A looks at activity 29. Student B looks at activity 49. Each student has a list of promises, threats and offers to make to his or her partner. The partner has to react, using the expressions given. For example:
A: If you like, I'll send you a postcard.
B: Lovely! Being sent postcards is nice. If we're not careful, someone will shout at us.
A: Oh dear, I don't like being shouted at.
and so on.
Encourage each pair to use a variety of the expressions given.

➤→ **Extra activity**

AS A CLASS, THEN IN PAIRS

Particularly in spoken English, *get* can sometimes be used as an auxiliary verb in place of *be*. It's usually used to refer to things that happen suddenly, unexpectedly or accidentally. For example:

The trees got blown down.
His leg got broken.
He got killed.

To give some practice in using *get* in this way, get the class to suggest as many natural or man-made disasters as they can think of and write them up on the board. The list might include:

earthquake, flood, thunderstorm, volcanic eruption, drought, etc.
car crash, explosion, riot, accident, war, battle, etc.

Then get each pair to write down a sentence describing one result of each of the disasters, following this pattern:

The building got damaged in the earthquake.
The driver got injured in the car crash.
13 people got drowned in the flood.
etc.

(There are more examples of *get* used in this way in the following exercise.)

Passive → Active → Passive

This exercise, which can be done in class or as homework, practises transforming sentences from active to passive and from passive to active.

The cold weather damaged the plants.
He broke his leg in a skiing accident.
The wind blew down dozens of trees.
The judges awarded her the prize.
The teacher threw him out of class for cheating.
The guide showed the party of tourists the sights.

The President was re-elected.
All the witnesses are being interviewed.
He's going to be given a big surprise.
My room hasn't been cleaned.
You will be told the results by my secretary.
I was given a video recorder for Christmas.

30 WORD FORMATION: Adjectives and adverbs

Summary

This is the first of four units on word formation. It might be best to intersperse them with other material in case they seem too indigestible as a 'four-course meal'.

Practice in forming and using adjectives with the suffixes *-y*, *-able*, *-al*, *-ive*, *-ful*, *-ish*:
> *woolly, cloudy, dusty, speedy, windy*, etc.
> *advisable, adorable, avoidable, readable*, etc.
> *chemical, habitual, functional, logical*, etc.
> *attractive, informative, explosive, persuasive*, etc.
> *careful, useful, painful, harmful*, etc.
> *youngish, reddish, tallish, greyish*, etc.

Forming antonyms of adjectives ending in *-ful*:
> *careless, useless, painless, harmless, thoughtless, meaningless, colourless, powerless, tuneless*
> *unhelpful, unsuccessful, untruthful, uneventful*

Forming adverbs with the suffix *-ly*:
> *slowly, carefully, painlessly, profitably*, etc.
> (but: *hard, fast, well, late, early*
> and: *in a lovely way, in a friendly way, in a silly way, in a lonely way*)

(*Practical English Usage* 12, 571)

Relevant errors

☆ Sheep are woollen animals.
☆ She is adoreable.
☆ We had a politic discussion.
☆ He worked hardly.
☆ He was successless.
☆ He is unthoughtful.
☆ He drives bad.
☆ He behaved sillily.

Forming adjectives

IN PAIRS AND/OR AS A CLASS

1 Allow time for study and questions.
2 Perhaps do this quickly with the whole class.
3 Check the answers and the spelling:
     acceptable, informative, logical, persuasive, regional, predictable,
     speedy, windy
4 This collocation exercise may be done by the whole class so that more
   ideas can be shared.

Point out that *-ible* is used instead of *-able* after *s* and *x*:
   possible, flexible, sensible (not to be confused with *sensitive*), *responsible,
   accessible*, etc.

Opposites

IN PAIRS AND/OR AS A CLASS

1 Make sure everyone understands.
2 Check everyone's spelling:
     *harmful/harmless, eventful/uneventful, painful/painless, powerful/
     powerless, tuneful/tuneless*
3 Again, this might be done with the whole class.

Point out that *-ful* can also be used to form nouns:
   a spoonful, a mouthful, a glassful, a cupful, etc.
and *-less* can be used to form other adjectives:
   homeless, childless, worthless, cloudless, etc.

Forming adverbs

IN GROUPS OF 3

Encourage the groups to suggest a variety of suitable adverbs and ask for the
best ideas at the end. The groups are not expected to restrict themselves to
adverbs exclusively: if they can express their ideas without using an adverb it
is nothing to worry about!
If necessary, offer some suggestions to uninspired groups:
   A good driver drives cautiously, reacts quickly, etc.
   A bad driver drives too fast, brakes suddenly, etc.
   A good student listens carefully, works hard, arrives punctually . . .
   *A bad student writes carelessly, arrives late, behaves in a silly
     way* . . .

A good friend listens patiently, helps you willingly . . .
An enemy talks about you unkindly, can't be trusted . . .
A good teacher speaks clearly, treats everyone fairly and equally, ends the
lesson punctually . . .
Listen for errors in using
   hard, fast, well
and
   in a silly way, in a friendly way, etc.

What's he or she like?

IN PAIRS

Get the pairs to find at least two adjectives or adverbs to describe each person.
Go round suggesting other suitable words they might use.

➡→   Extra activity

Ask the members of the class, working alone or in pairs or as homework, to
write a paragraph on one of these topics:
   Describe yourself *or*
   Describe an experience you remember well (true or fictional),
using 10 of the adjectives and adverbs from this unit.

Fill in the gaps

This exercise is deliberately woolly as it is designed to get students to search
through the lists for suitable adjectives. There are several possibilities for
some of the sentences and these answers are suggestions only:

Sheep are *adorable* creatures.
Careful – that antique bowl is *breakable!*
Dr Jekyll drank the *colourless* liquid.
Prof. White has *greyish* hair.
The President is a*n untruthful* man.
I find electronic music very *repetitive.*
She is a *habitual* nail-biter.
I found the story very *enjoyable.*
I'm afraid they write rather *carelessly.*
I hope you're *successful* in the exam.

31 WORD FORMATION: Verbs

Summary

Practice in forming and using common 'causative verbs' with the suffix *-en* and in using other common causative verbs:
> to *tighten* (= to make something tight), to *loosen*, to *flatten*, etc.
> to *cool*, to *clean*, to *raise*, to *purify*, to *enlarge*, etc.

Forming and using verbs with the prefix *un-* and in using some common phrasal verbs with the particle *up*:
> to *undo*, to *unscrew*, to *uncover*, to *unzip*, etc.
> to *do up*, to *screw up*, to *cover up*, to *zip up*, etc.

Forming and using verbs with the prefixes *over-* and *mis-*:
> to *overeat*, to *overwork*, to *oversleep*, etc.
> to *misunderstand*, to *misjudge*, to *misbehave*, etc.

(For a complete list of the verbs, see the Student's Book.)

Relevant errors

☆ He tighted his belt.
☆ They strongened the bridge.
☆ They were missbehaving.

☆ She heatened the soup.
☆ They want to rise the Titanic.

Make it tighter!

IN PAIRS

The answers given are suggestions only.

1 I didn't mean to *frighten* you. Sorry.
   This dress needs to be *shortened*.
   Could someone *sharpen* this knife for me?
   The building was *flattened* by the explosion.
   The sauce tastes nice but it needs to be *thickened*.

>>>→

2 This part introduces some more causative verbs that may cause problems. The suffix *-en* is only used to form some causative verbs, not all of them.

The food's ready, it only needs *heating*.

They used steel bars to *strengthen* the wall.

I really ought to *clean* my shoes.

Use these tablets to *purify* the water.

I can't *lift* this sofa all by myself.

After the ceremony the flag was *lowered/raised*.

The text has been *simplified* for foreign students.

When the pairs have finished the exercise, get them to test each other like this:
A: He made it flat?
B: He flattened it! He made it hot?
A: He heated it!
and so on.
Alternatively, do this yourself with the whole class.

Do it again!

IN PAIRS

I'd like you to *retype* this letter.

It's high time my flat was *redecorated*.

He took the radio to pieces but then he couldn't *reassemble* it.

We were all surprised when she *remarried* at the age of 85.

A Christmas tree can sometimes be *replanted* in your garden.

The book's so popular that it's been *reprinted* six times.

Again, get the pairs to test each other at the end:
A: She did it again?
B: She redid it. She thought about it again?
A: She rethought it.
and so on.
Or do this with the whole class yourself instead.

Use your imagination . . .

IN GROUPS OF 3

Emphasise that the 'best' groups will come up with the most answers, and that the 'worst' will probably be the first ones to finish. To start the ball rolling, ask the whole class to suggest some of the things that you can unbutton and what may happen if you overeat:

You can unbutton an overcoat, or a shirt, or a blouse, or a pair of trousers, or a raincoat, etc.

If you overeat you may get too fat, you may become overweight, you may feel sick, you may make yourself ill, you may become unhealthy, etc.

Did you understand correctly?

IN PAIRS

Note that the verbs need to be rearranged in this exercise!

misbehave — It doesn't normally matter if you *mispronounce* a word in English.

miscalculate — He crashed because he *misjudged* the other car's speed.

misinform — As usual, the children have been *misbehaving*.

misjudge — No, I'm not resigning. You must have been *misinformed*.

misread — I'm sorry, I think I *misunderstood* the instructions you gave us.

mispronounce — She missed the train because she *misread* the timetable.

misunderstand — They *miscalculated* the amount of money they had spent.

▶→ **Extra activity**

Get the class to suggest what you're pretending to do as you *mime* a number
of the verbs from this unit. For example:

Teacher   (mimes lifting something)
Class: You're lifting something. Or raising something. Are you lifting a
             suitcase?
Teacher   (mimes lowering something)
Class: Are you lowering it now?
and so on.

There is absolutely no need to be 'good' at miming for this activity. Indeed, an
ambiguous or unclear mime may be much more productive than a profession-
ally performed one. It is a good idea, however, to prepare for this activity
beforehand by looking through the verbs in the unit and noting down the
ones you think you can mime reasonably well.

Complete the sentences

Vegetables taken from the freezer should not be *refrozen.*

The palace was burnt down in the war and later it was *rebuilt.*

The dam burst because it had been *weakened* by the earthquake.

I can't *unscrew* the lid of this jar of jam.

Excuse me, waiter, I think you've *overcharged* us for the wine.

If you continue *overworking* you may end up in hospital.

The committee was asked to *reconsider* its decision.

The ship was firmly stuck on the rocks and couldn't be *refloated.*

I'm afraid there has been a slight *misunderstanding.*

32 WORD FORMATION: Abstract nouns

Summary

Practice in forming and using nouns formed from adjectives with the suffixes
-ness, -ity, -ence and *-y*:
  happiness, politeness, tidiness, cleverness, etc.
  stupidity, certainty, maturity, popularity, etc.
  violence, intelligence, patience, confidence, etc.
  honesty, anxiety, accuracy, sympathy, etc.

Forming and using nouns related to other common adjectives:
  strong – strength, true – truth, bored – boredom, brave – bravery, etc.

Forming and using nouns formed from verbs with the suffixes *-ment, -ion, -ation, -ance, -ence* and *-al*:
  announcement, punishment, excitement, etc.
  discussion, suspicion, opposition, etc.
  admiration, pronunciation, explanation, etc.
  performance, disappearance, assistance, etc.
  insistence, preference, persistence, etc.
  refusal, survival, arrival, etc.

(For complete lists, see the Student's Book.)

Relevant errors

☆ I can't stand stupidness.
☆ He's good at organisement.
☆ What's the deepness of the pool?
☆ It's your choose!

Adjectives → nouns

IN PAIRS

1 Watch everyone's spelling. The key to this exercise is in communication activity 40 in the Student's Book. Don't let the pairs know this until they have either finished or reached as far as they can manage in the time available.

2 Again, correct spelling is likely to be a problem. Encourage each pair to use a dictionary (preferably an English-to-English one, such as the *Longman Dictionary of Contemporary English*), rather than to call on you.

   The key to this part is in activity 55 in the Student's Book.

3 She's blushing because of her *shyness*.

   I enjoy the *responsibility* of my new job.

   There's too much *violence* on TV.

   The Thames is 346 km in *length*.

   I swear to you that I'm telling the *truth*.

   He suffers from *nervousness* before an exam.

   Pandas are protected because of their *rarity*.

   I love dogs because of their *loyalty*.

   You might at least show some *sympathy*.

   These exercises will increase your *strength*.

   I believe in *equality* between men and women.

   Teachers are said to need a lot of *patience*.

At the end, go through the harder ones in the lists again with the whole class like this:

Teacher: Polite?
Class: Politeness!
Teacher: Sympathetic?
Class: Sympathy!
and so on.

Verbs → nouns

IN PAIRS

1 The key to this part is in activity 52. Don't let the class know this until they have all had a good go at the exercise.
2 Discourage students from using you as a walking dictionary. They should use a real one for preference. The key to this part is in activity 30 in the Student's Book.

3 We were given a warm *reception*.

   The pianist gave a wonderful *performance*.

   I hope I've made the right *choice*.

   I didn't understand the *explanation*.

   He couldn't understand my *pronunciation*.

   They have no *proof* of his guilt.

Allow him to speak without *interruption*.
I'd like to make a serious *complaint*.
In *comparison* with him, she's a genius.
They celebrated the *birth* of their 7th son.
The expedition ended in complete *failure*.
She asked her parents' *permission* to get married.
They had no *suspicion* that he was the thief.
Thanks for your kind *assistance*.
To my *embarrassment* I had forgotten my wallet.
To our *astonishment* he had forgotten the date.
The children were on their best *behaviour*.
The whole show was a great *success*.

At the end go through the lists again with the class, getting them to shout out
the appropriate nouns:
Teacher: Arrive?
Class: Arrival.
Teacher: Laugh?
Class: Laughter.
and so on.
Alternatively, the pairs can do this together with one looking at the lists while
the other looks away from or covers up the lists.

➤→ Extra activity

Get the members of the class to write a story using as many nouns, verbs or
adjectives from this unit as they can. It could be a description of a person they
like or admire, a narrative featuring a well-known historical figure, or a
description of a film or book they have enjoyed. Perhaps put a limit of just 10
words to be incorporated in the story.

33 WORD FORMATION: Opposites

Summary

Practice in forming and using negative adjectives, nouns and verbs with the prefixes *un-*, *in-*, *im-*, *il-*, *ir-* and *non-*:
    unlikely, uncomfortable, unmarried, unsafe, etc.
    inaccurate, incapable, intolerant, etc.
    impossible, imperfect, immoral, etc.   (before *p* or *m*)
    illegal, illogical, illegible, etc.   (before *l*)
    irregular, irrational, irrelevant, etc.   (before *r*)
    non-drip, non-stick, non-smoker, etc.

Using antonyms of some common adjectives:
    happy – sad, warm – cool, gentle – rough, tame – wild, etc.

(For complete lists, see the Student's Book.)

Relevant errors

☆ This is unpossible.
☆ This is inrelevant.
☆ You're being unarrogant.
☆ Don't be so unmodest.

Negative forms

IN PAIRS

1 Allow time for study and questions. Point out that *un-* is by far the most common and flexible of all the prefixes.

2 Check the answers:

> *disadvantage, uncertain, uncommon, inconvenient, incorrect, unfit, unfriendly, unkind, ungrateful, dishonest, unready, unripe, insincere*

3 This chair is rather *uncomfortable*.
The result of the match was *unpredictable*.
My old car is rather *unreliable*.
Their behaviour *displeases* their parents.
I *disapprove* of smoking in restaurants.
They seem rather *intolerant* of foreigners.
They look alike but in fact they're *unrelated*.
She is *unlikely* to pass the test.
After the accident he was *unconscious*.
Eating *unripe* fruit is bad for you.

4 Allow more time for study and questions.

5 Large hotels can be very *impersonal*.
The point he made seems *irrelevant* to me.
The library contains mostly *non-fiction* books.
He is a passionate *anti-smoker*.
40% of the population are *illiterate*.
Her signature was *illegible*.

Finally, go through the words that may have caused problems in these exercises, putting each into a sentence, and get the class to call out the appropriate negative forms:
Teacher: Was he able to do it?
Class: No, he was unable to do it!
Teacher: Was the chair comfortable?
Class: No, it was uncomfortable.
Teacher: Is he a smoker?
Class: No, he's a non-smoker.
and so on.

What's the opposite of . . . ?

IN PAIRS

1 Go round helping and making suggestions. When everyone has finished, announce that the right answers are all in activity 42 near the end of the Student's Book. Allow time for checking spelling.

2 This part can be done with the whole class making suggestions. It will be found that all the adjectives can be used in some fairly common collocations. ⟫→

3 I waited for my soup to get *cool*.
   He was too *mean* to lend me the money.
   I can't eat this bread, it's too *stale*.
   I'm not tired, I'm *wide awake*.
   The Japanese like to eat *raw* fish.
   Is it *safe* to cross the river?
   Yes, the river's very *shallow*.
   1,000 people were *present* at the meeting.
   I prefer to stay in *expensive* hotels.
   I had flu last week but now I'm *well* again.

Finally, get the pairs to 'test' each other on the opposites with one looking at
the lists and the other looking away.

➡→ Extra activity 🖎

IN PAIRS

Get the class to pick out the 10 words from this unit that they think are *both*
useful *and* hard to remember. Then, in pairs, they should write 10 sentences
using the selected words.

Complete the sentences 🖎

This exercise calls for the use of words from units 32 and 33.

The audience expressed their *disapproval* by booing and whistling.
Marks will be deducted in the exam for grammatical *inaccuracy*.
She frowned at them to show her *displeasure*.
The father was imprisoned for his *cruelty* to the children.
The dog was beaten by its owner for its *disobedience*.
I can't predict the results of the election with any *certainty*.
After our *disagreement* we are no longer on speaking terms.
We wish to apologise to passengers for any *inconvenience* caused by the
   strike.
The children held each other tight for *warmth*.
I'm sorry about the *untidiness* of my desk.

34 QUANTITY AND NUMBERS

Summary

Practice in using appropriate expressions to describe one item of 'uncountable nouns':
   a piece of work, a pot of tea, a jar of honey, a slice of cake, etc.

Distinguishing between 'countable' and 'uncountable' nouns:
   traffic, information, money, homework, honey, etc.   (uncountable)
   car(s), fact(s), pound(s), exercise(s), bee(s), etc.   (countable)

Using *much* and *many* accurately:
   How much time is there left?
   How many hours will it take?
   He's got so much time that he can stop for tea on the way.
   There were so many people there that the police couldn't control them.

Understanding and using numbers (spoken aloud at normal speed), and saying numbers clearly and confidently:
   'four, fourteen, forty, forty-four, four hundred and forty four, four thousand four hundred and forty-four, forty-four thousand four hundred and . . . ' etc.

Doing simple arithmetic in English and saying the sums aloud:
   $4 \times 4 = 16$ *'four times/multiplied by four equals sixteen'*
   $2 + 2 = 4$ *'two plus/and two equals/makes four'*
   $4 \div 2$ *'four divided by two'*
   $4 - 2$ *'four minus two'*
   11^2 *'eleven squared'*

(*Practical English Usage* 163, 393, 560, 434, 435, 436)

Relevant errors

☆ Can you give me an information?
☆ I'd like some informations.
☆ I'd like a box of runny honey.
☆ What a lovely sunshine!

☆ Forteen men
☆ Fourty men
☆ Four hundred forty-four
Misunderstanding numbers

How much? How many?

IN PAIRS

1 This exercise deals with quantifying 'uncountable' nouns

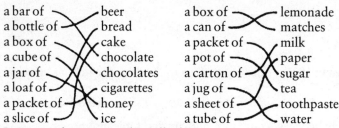

a bar of	beer	a box of	lemonade
a bottle of	bread	a can of	matches
a box of	cake	a packet of	milk
a cube of	chocolate	a pot of	paper
a jar of	chocolates	a carton of	sugar
a loaf of	cigarettes	a jug of	tea
a packet of	honey	a sheet of	toothpaste
a slice of	ice	a tube of	water

Point out that we can also talk about:
a piece of chocolate (or *a square*)
a spoonful of sugar (or *a kilo*)
a pint of beer (or *a glass* or *can*) etc.
Ask for similar suggestions for the other 'uncountables' listed.

2 Student A looks at activity 28. Student B looks at activity 53. The pairs imagine that they are on a camping holiday together and have dwindling stocks of provisions. They have to find out from each other how much or how many of every item they have got left. This pattern for the conversation is given in the communication activity:
A: Have you got any salt left?
B: Yes. How much would you like?   *OR*   How many packets would you like?
A: Two, please.
B: I'm sorry, I've only got one (packet).   *OR*   Here you are!

So much! So many!

IN PAIRS

This exercise looks at countable and uncountable nouns that are normally used to refer to similar ideas. (One can of course count one's money, but only by saying '£1, £2, £3' not '1 money, 2 moneys, 3 moneys'.)
so much advice / so many suggestions
so much information / so many facts
so much research / so many experiments
so many armchairs / so much furniture
so much homework / so many exercises
so much luggage / so many bags

so many reports / so much news
so much knowledge / so many references

During our holiday we had *so much sunshine that we got very brown.*

The students in this class have made *so much progress that they'll all pass the exam.*

There was *so much traffic that it took three hours to get there.*

In English there seems to be *so much vocabulary that I'll never be able to learn it all.*

Similar 'uncountable' nouns that may cause confusion are:
hair, weather, behaviour, work, health, travel, pasta, spaghetti
Note also that some nouns are (perhaps unexpectedly) 'plural' in English:

The police are . . .	*A lot of us are . . .*
People are . . .	*The majority of us are . . .*
A number of us are . . .	*A group of us are . . .*

while others are (perhaps unexpectedly) 'singular':

The news is . . .	*A series of disasters has . . .*
Measles is . . .	*The United States is . . .*
Politics is . . .	*Mathematics is . . .*

and yet others are either singular or plural interchangeably:

The whole class is/are . . .	*The government is/are . . .*
The orchestra is/are . . .	*The company is/are . . .*
My family is/are . . .	*Our team is/are . . .*

Finally, note also the following irregular plurals:
2 sheep, 3 aircraft, 4 fish, 5 deer, 6 children, 7 mice, 8 feet, 9 teeth, 10 geese.

How many can you count?

IN PAIRS

First of all, draw this diagram on the board and ask how many squares there are in it. The answer is **5** (4 small ones and one big one). This sets the scene for the activity in the Student's Book, where students have to count *aloud* the number of sides, squares and triangles.

The right answers are, reading from the left: **26, 30** (16 tiny squares; 9 small ones, each containing 4 tiny ones; 4 large ones, each containing 4 tiny ones; and one very big one containing all the tiny ones), **35** (10 small ones, 10 medium ones containing 2 small ones each, 5 large ones containing 3 small ones each, 5 large ones containing 2 small ones plus the central pentagon, 5 large pointed ones containing 4 small ones plus the central pentagon), and **27** (9 tiny ones, 4 small ones containing 4 tiny ones each, 9 medium ones, 4 large ones containing 4 medium ones each, one huge one).

Confused students may need help from others who counted accurately.

High numbers

IN PAIRS

This activity should be done at speed: it is basically a pronunciation exercise. Partners should take it in turns like this:

A: Two terrified tourists.

B: Twenty-two terrified tourists.

A: Two hundred and twenty-two terrified tourists.

B: Two thousand two hundred and twenty-two terrified tourists.

and so on.

Afterwards the partners can try to catch each other out by pointing to various numbers shown and challenging each other to say them aloud:

A (points to 6,666)

B: Six thousand six hundred and . . . er . . . sixty-six.

▶→ Extra activity

AS A CLASS

Get the class to sit in one large circle (or square or polygon). If this is unwieldy, several smaller circles can be formed. Each student writes down a 4-digit number within a simple sentence. For example:

'*1,373 Italians entered the race.*'

'*9,837 Frenchmen blocked the motorway.*'

Then each student says his or her sentence to the person on the left, who should note down the number before repeating the whole sentence to the next person. At the end, the sentences that return to their originators may have got quite distorted!

Arithmetic 🃏

IN PAIRS

This activity is not a maths test and requires no special knowledge of arithmetic really. Make sure to begin with that everyone knows how to say these symbols aloud:

×   *'multiplied by'* or *'times'*
+   *'plus'* or *'and'*
−   *'minus'*
÷   *'divided by'*
=   *'equals'*

Before starting the communication activity, get the class to follow these instructions:

Teacher: Start with 4. Add 16. How much is that? 20, right. Divide that by 2 . . . Plus 15 . . . Minus 1 . . . Divide by 12 . . . Multiply that by 2 . . . And what's the answer?

Class: 4!

Then, working in pairs, Student A looks at activity 16 while B looks at 45. Each then gets the other to do some more calculations, using a pencil, paper and even a calculator if available.

Fill the gaps

IN PAIRS

One new symbol here is: 11^2 ('eleven squared').
The pairs are supposed to guess or deduce the missing numbers, not try to do the long multiplication!

3 *times* 37 equals 111.

If you *divide* 222 by 37, you get 6.

If you *multiply* 37 by 9, the answer is 333.

37 × 12 *equals* 444.

37 × 15 *equals 555.*

37 × 18 *equals 666.*

$11^2 = 121.$

$111^2 = 12,321$

$1,111^2 = 1,234,321$

$11,111^2 = 123,454,321$

$111,111^2 = 12,345,654,321$

$1,111,111^2 =$
    12,345,678,987,654,321

35 JOINING SENTENCES I

Summary

This is the first of three units on forming complex sentences and joining two sentences, using conjunctions and 'discourse markers'.

Practice in using *when* with appropriate verb forms:
> *I spoke to him when he arrived.*
> *I'll speak to him when he arrives.*
> *I had finished lunch when he arrived.*
> *I had my dinner when he went.*   (straight after)
> *I had my dinner when he had gone.*   (straight after or some time after)

Using other time-conjunctions appropriately:
> *as, until/till, by the time, whenever, soon after, before, since, as soon as, once, while*

e.g. *He rang me before I had breakfast.*
> *I used to cry whenever I was spoken to.*
> *We'll all be very hungry by the time he arrives.*

Using time-prepositions:
> *before, after, since, during, till/until*
> *He rang me before breakfast.*

e.g. *We'll have to wait till his arrival.*

Forming complex sentences using time-conjunctions and time-prepositions:
> *While he was watching the match, he began to feel sick.*
> *After I had reported the theft of my passport, I found it behind a cupboard.*
> *During the evening, while I was reading some letters, I had a phone call.*

(*Practical English Usage* 29, 467, 245, 187, 188, 216, 84)

Relevant errors

☆ While I had watched TV he phoned me.
☆ During I was watching TV he phoned me.
☆ I'm watching TV since 8 o'clock.
☆ After that I recognised him, I said hallo.
☆ I'll speak to him when he will arrive.

ANY OR ALL OF THE EXERCISES IN THIS UNIT CAN BE DONE
IN WRITING.

When . . .

IN PAIRS

It may be necessary to point out that the exercise forms a story and that *when* means 'after', 'as soon as' or 'at the same time as'.

When he heard the phone ringing, *he was having a shower.*
When he got to the phone, *it (had) stopped ringing.*
When it rang again, *he got to it in time.*
When he heard his fiancée's voice, *he felt apprehensive.*
When she told him the news, *he was speechless.*
When he had got over the shock, *he started shouting at her over the phone.*
When he put down the receiver, *he sat down and poured himself a stiff drink.*
When the phone rang again later, *he ignored it and let it ring.*
When we saw him the next morning, *he had recovered from the shock and was feeling quite cheerful.*

What did his fiancée say to him?

Rearrange the sentences

IN PAIRS

This activity introduces some time-conjunctions that will be used later in the unit.

I held my breath — until I had finished all my work.
I didn't leave the room — when I'd saved up enough money.
I bought a new coat — as the door slowly opened.
I used to get into trouble — by the time she came back.
I forgot to wash my hands — till they arrived.
I sent the parcel — whenever I came home late.
I had eaten all her chocolates — soon after I heard the exam results.
I went on holiday — before I had dinner.
I waited patiently — as soon as I found out the address.
I was able to do the exercise — once I'd found the answers in the back.

Complete the sentences

IN PAIRS

. . . while we were watching the programme.
. . . after the programme had finished.
. . . until we went to bed.
. . . since I saw Superman III.

The second half of the exercise requires the use of time-prepositions, which can be used with a noun or with *-ing*:
. . . before lunch.
. . . before having lunch.

. . . during the night.
. . . after waking up.
. . . till daybreak/dawn.
. . . since my childhood.

Another time-preposition is *by* (equivalent to the time-conjunction *by the time*) and its use may cause some problems:
Please do this by lunchtime.
Please do this by the time I get back.
The meaning of the sentences above is slightly different from:
Please do this before lunchtime.
Please do this before I get back.
Often *by* and *by the time* imply the idea of a deadline or ultimatum. Compare, for example:
I want an answer by tomorrow. (= today or at the latest tomorrow)
I want an answer before tomorrow. (= today and not tomorrow)

Fill the gaps

ALONE OR IN PAIRS

He'd smoked 20 cigarettes *by the time* it was his turn to speak.
They gave us the results *after* we'd been waiting for two hours.
The survivors waited 24 hours *until* they were rescued.
I haven't laughed so much *since* Father fell into the river.
I try to do plenty of revision *before* I take an exam.
He took his coat and hat off *as soon as* he came into the house.
They waited in silence *until* the policeman had gone past.
You shouldn't have called to her *while* she was crossing the road.

Discuss any variations with the class.

Late for work again!

IN PAIRS

Another story:

I read my mail before *leaving the house/I left the house.*
I walked to the bus stop after *I had read my letters.*
I had to queue at the stop till *the bus came.*
I read the paper while *I was waiting for the bus to come.*
I'd been waiting for half an hour by the time *the bus came.*
I continued reading the paper during *the journey.*
I jumped off the bus as soon as *it got to my stop.*
I got some dirty looks from everyone in the office when *I walked in at 10 o'clock – late again!*

➤→ Extra activity

Get the members of the class to write a paragraph telling the very beginning or the very end of a well-known tale or story (e.g. Cinderella, Jack and the Beanstalk, or a national folk-tale) in their own words, using time-conjunctions and time-prepositions as appropriate. Let students see each other's work afterwards and make comments.

Join the sentences

Variations are possible from the model answers given here:

While he has been at college, he seems to have learned nothing.
After I had reported the theft of my passport, I discovered it in my suitcase.
After I had paid £200 for a suit, I saw the same one at half the price.
Until he told me he was your brother, I had no idea who he was.
I did a lot of work after I'd decided to take the phone off the hook.
She tried to apologise after she'd been terribly rude to me.
As soon as she saw it was raining, she rushed into the garden to get the washing. ⟫→

145

Before you leave the house, make sure you lock the door.
After you've finished this exercise you can have a well-earned
  rest.

36 JOINING SENTENCES II

Summary

Practice in using conjunctions to show conditions, results, reasons, causes, purposes, precautions and contrasts:
> *in case, because, as, although, even though, so that, if, as long as, provided that, unless*

e.g. *I've brought my umbrella in case it rains.* (precaution)
> *I've got my umbrella up because/as it's raining.* (reason)
> *You don't need an umbrella unless it's raining.* (condition)

Using co-ordinating structures:
> *both . . . and*
> *neither . . . nor*
> *either . . . or*
> *none of . . . except*

e.g. *Both Bill and his sister have red hair.*
> *None of the members of his family except his brother have freckles.*

(*Practical English Usage* 153, 316, 610, 100, 83, 310)

Relevant errors

☆ I've brought my umbrella if it rains.
☆ Although I don't like him, but I find him charming.
☆ Both they like her and her sister.
☆ I don't eat neither fish nor meat.

ANY OR ALL OF THE EXERCISES IN THIS UNIT CAN BE DONE IN WRITING. 📝

Just in case

IN PAIRS

Discuss any variations from the suggested answers below.

He's brought an umbrella *in case* it rains later.   ⟫→

He's wearing a hat *because* he doesn't want us to know he's bald.
He's going to bed with a hot water bottle *although* it's midsummer.
The town was flooded *because* it had rained so heavily.
I've brought some sandwiches *in case* I feel hungry.
I didn't go to bed *even though* I had an awful cold.
I have to wear glasses *so that* I can see to read.
You can teach me to drive *as long as* you promise not to lose your temper.
I won't speak to her again *unless* she apologises.
I'm going dancing tonight *even though* my ankle's swollen.

In other words

IN PAIRS

Point out the equivalence of the prepositions with the conjunctions. Perhaps see where similar prepositions can be used in the previous exercise:
e.g. *He's brought an umbrella in case of rain.*

We went swimming despite the rain. Although *it was raining, we went swimming.*
The trains were late due to bad weather. Because the weather *was bad, the trains were late.*
He broke the teapot because of his clumsiness. Because *he was clumsy, he broke the teapot.*
They passed the test in spite of their laziness. Even though *they were lazy, they passed the test.*
She left early so as to catch her train. She left early so that *she could catch her train.*
I lost my temper due to their stupid behaviour. As *they were behaving stupidly, I lost my temper.*

Both . . . and . . .

IN GROUPS OF 4

1 Sentences can be made up about both the horizontal and the vertical rows in the chart.

2 If preferred, students may discuss their likes and dislikes of some different local dishes and drinks. Or perhaps different sports or entertainments.

3 Check the written sentences for accuracy.

Other useful structures here are:
Anne likes meat and so does Charles.
Charles doesn't like rice and neither does Anne.

➡➤ Extra activity

IN GROUPS OF 4

This activity is more suitable for a more advanced class. Using a similar chart of likes and dislikes (about hobbies, sports or pastimes), this activity gives practice in using:
not only . . . but also

This is sometimes an easy structure to use:
He not only likes beer but also wine.
He likes not only beer but also wine.
Not only Bob but also Ben likes beer.

But it is tricky to use at the beginning of a sentence:
Not only does he like beer but also wine.
Not only have I drunk your beer but I've also eaten your sandwich.

Get each group to find out about each other's likes and dislikes, so that they can write sentences like these:
John likes not only football but also tennis.
Not only does John like football but also tennis.
Not only John but also Bill plays football.
etc.

Keep a careful check on word order and the correct use of inversion.

Uncles 〖✖〗

IN PAIRS

Student A should look at activity 23. Student B should look at activity 54. Each student has complete cartoons of only three of the uncles. They have to describe their uncles so that their partner can draw in the missing details, using these structures given in the communication activity:
Both Uncle Dave and Uncle Eric . . .
Neither Uncle Eric nor Uncle Frank . . .
Uncle Dave hasn't got either a . . . or a . . .

And, but . . .

IN PAIRS

This transformation exercise shows some of the different meanings of *and*, *but* and *or*.

He rang up his friend because he felt depressed.
I'm going to stay up although it's past my bedtime.
You'll get into trouble if you do that again.
Neither my father nor my mother smokes.
I'm going to work even though I'm feeling ill.
You won't get better unless you go to bed.
I love both oranges and grapefruit.

Rewrite the sentences

As Ann and Tim were waiting for the same flight, they started talking.
She was feeling very hungry because she hadn't had breakfast.
Being so hungry she accepted his offer of a sandwich.
They got on so well because of their common interest in music.
They both enjoyed playing the piano.
Although she was much older than him, he found her very attractive.
Even though they had a big row the next day, they decided to get married.
He enjoyed both her cooking and her company.
He never let her go out alone so that she couldn't meet any other men.

37 JOINING SENTENCES III: Links between sentences

Summary

Practice in using time adverbs to join two sentences 'across a full stop':
Before that, Earlier ...
After that, Afterwards, Later ...
Meanwhile, At the same time ...
e.g. *He left punctually at 6. Before that we'd had along talk.*
    They had a lovely time at the dance. Meanwhile I was at home working.

Using adverbial phrases showing results, contrasts, reasons, conditions and alternatives to join two sentences 'across a full stop':
That's why, Therefore ...
Nevertheless, Nonetheless ...
Otherwise ...
Alternatively, On the other hand ...
However ...
e.g. *I hate bananas. That's why I never eat fruit salad.*
    I love oranges. Nevertheless I hate having to peel them.

Using 'discourse markers' to join two sentences 'across a full stop':
Unfortunately ...
Fortunately, Luckily ...
Funnily enough, Strangely enough, Believe it or not ...
Actually, In actual fact, Really, of course ...
In other words, That is to say ...
e.g. *It was raining heavily. Luckily, I had my umbrella.*
    This work is not up to scratch. In other words, it's appalling.

Using 'discourse markers' to connect sentences in a paragraph:

In the first place ...	*In the second place ...*	*Lastly ...*
To begin with ...	*Secondly ...*	*Finally ...*
First of all ...	*What's more ...*	*For example ...*
One reason ...	*Another reason ...*	*For instance ...*
	Moreover ...	

e.g. *One reason why joining sentences is difficult is that there are so many different conjunctions and adverbs used. Another reason is that the underlying ideas are often complex. Moreover, in a foreign language, expressing such ideas can be tricky. For instance, if you want to ...*

(*Practical English Usage* 29, 172)

Relevant errors

☆ He fell into the river after that he was rescued.
☆ Nevertheless I like opera. I hate orchestral music.
☆ He fell into the sea luckily. He was rescued.
☆ Secondly I admire his work. First of all I liked him as a person.

ANY OR ALL OF THE EXERCISES IN THIS UNIT CAN BE DONE
IN WRITING. 🖎

Time adverbs

IN PAIRS

The adverbs and adverbial phrases practised in this exercise and in the rest of the unit are likely to be most useful to students in their writing. Such expressions are needed to produce coherent letters and compositions.

He ate two dozen oysters. *Afterwards* he had a terrible stomachache.

I'm going off to play a round of golf. *Meanwhile* I'd like you to get on with the work.

They spent the night on the mountain. *Earlier* I'd warned them not to go up there.

We assumed a burglar had broken the window. *Later* we found nothing was missing.

I waited and waited for her to arrive. *Meanwhile* she was stuck in the lift.

The washing got soaked in the rain. *Later* the sun came out and dried it all.

Over 30 people came to the party. *Earlier* we'd only bought enough food for about 10.

Note that a comma can be used after many of these adverbs (and after the 'discourse markers' in later exercises). However, its use is optional as it is used to make the meaning of a sentence clearer, not because of any fixed rules.

Perhaps point out the slight difference between:
    Before that   (= shortly before, even immediately before)
and   *Earlier*   (= some time before)
    After that/Afterwards   (= shortly after)
and   *Later*   (= some time after)
    Meanwhile   (= in the meantime *or* simultaneously)
and   *At the same time*   (= simultaneously).

Reason, contrast, result

IN PAIRS

After the pairs have completed the exercise and checked their results, get them to 'test' each other's memories on this and the previous exercise. This can be done by covering up the central columns where the adverbs have been written and trying to remember what is now concealed. Alternatively, you could do this with the whole class.

You can go by plane. *Alternatively,* if that scares you, you can take the train.

Don't forget to take your passport. *Otherwise* you won't be allowed to cross the frontier.

English people are said to be reserved. *However* that applies only to people in the South.

I knew it was probably going to rain. *Nonetheless* I decided to go out for a walk.

If you wait for me I'll give you a lift – *otherwise* you'll have to walk all the way.

I knew the plane would be delayed. *That's why* I brought a book to read.

I don't normally like thrillers. *However* the one I'm reading now is really good.

We can have French or Spanish food. *On the other hand* we could go to the Italian restaurant.

I know television is a waste of time. *Nevertheless* I often enjoy watching it.

It's a good idea to write down new words. *Otherwise* you're likely to forget them.

Unfortunately . . .

IN PAIRS

This exercise merely scratches the surface of the use of 'discourse markers' (practised also in unit 22: 'On the one hand . . . '). To learn to use such expressions appropriately and fluently takes a lot of time. It depends on experience of reading different kinds of texts and needs encouraging in composition practice.

They fell into the sea. *Unfortunately* neither of them could swim.

I discovered that I'd got no cash with me. *Luckily,* I had my credit card.

⟫→

It was nice to see her again. *Believe it or not,* we last met when I was still
at school.

The party didn't go all that well. *Actually* it was a complete disaster.

I was looking forward to the show. *Unfortunately* I wasn't able to go.

There wasn't much to eat or drink. *In fact* there were only sandwiches and
beer.

He can't speak a word of English. *Strangely enough* he speaks fluent
Japanese.

The murderer was sent to prison. *Unfortunately* he escaped and hasn't
been recaptured.

He spoke too fast and in a strange accent. *In other words* we couldn't
understand him at all.

The robbers tied her up and locked her in the cellar. *Fortunately* she
managed to escape.

The reasons why . . .

IN PAIRS (or possibly in groups of 4 – see below)

Many of the 'discourse markers' here are particularly useful in spoken
English as well as in writing paragraphs.

Student A should look at activity 25. Student B should look at activity 50.
Each student is given several points to make about a number of different
controversial topics. The idea is to make these points, using the expressions
given. Allow some time for thinking before each short discussion begins.

If this seems too difficult an exercise for a particular class to handle in
pairs, it can be done in groups of four with two students sharing the information in the communication activity and supporting each other in the
discussions.

➤➔ Extra activity

IN PAIRS

To give further practice in using 'discourse markers' in writing paragraphs
(as required, for example, in First Certificate Use of English: Section B), get
the pairs to select one of the topics they discussed in the previous activity and
write two paragraphs together. One paragraph should give the pros and the
other the cons of the topic.

Write two paragraphs

Both of these paragraphs should be done so as to give practice in using both sets of 'discourse markers' introduced on page 74 of the Student's Book. Get the students to read each other's completed paragraphs and comment on them.

38 PHRASAL AND PREPOSITIONAL VERBS I

Summary

Practice in recognising the difference between a 'phrasal verb' and a 'prepositional verb' and the concomitant differences in sentence structure:

PHRASAL VERBS	PREPOSITIONAL VERBS / VERBS + PREPOSITION
I put on[1] my coat.	*Sandals don't go with[2] a suit.*
I put my coat on[1].	*Sandals don't go with[2] it.*
I put it on[1].	*(*Sandals don't go it with.)*
(*I put on it.)	*(*Sandals don't go a suit with.)*
He jumped off[1].	*He jumped off[2] the cliff.*
	He jumped off[2] it.

[1] these are adverbial particles [2] these are prepositions
  *incorrect word order

Using common adverbial particles with verbs of motion as phrasal verbs with literal (non-idiomatic) meanings:

VERBS	ADVERBIAL PARTICLES
come go get climb	*away back*
bring take carry	*past by over round*
pull push	*out off on*
run walk drive ride	*up down in out*
jump fall	

e.g. *Please go away and don't come back.*
  They ran away when they saw me come in.

Using some common idiomatic prepositional verbs:
  see through, feel like, work on, look for, look after, send for, make for, ask for, take after, go with, look like, stand for, get used to, call for
e.g. *I saw through his disguise.*
  I'm working on a new book.

Replacing formal-style verbs with colloquial phrasal and prepositional verbs:
  remove – take off, raise – lift up, regard – look on, request – ask for, etc.
e.g. *He removed his coat.*   *He took off his coat.*
  He raised his hand.   *He lifted his hand up.*

(*Practical English Usage* 491, 492)

Relevant errors

☆ She ran the hill down.
☆ He wrote down it.
☆ Quick, extinguish the fire!
☆ Our new baby looks after her grandmother.

Some easy phrasal verbs

IN PAIRS

This exercise is designed to reassure students that phrasal verbs are not as formidable as they're sometimes painted and that many of them have an easily-understood literal meaning.

Begin by going through the adverbial particles and their meanings. Perhaps refer back to the similar exercise in unit 9: 'Run, walk or fly'.

Many of the verbs and adverbial particles can be mimed by the teacher or, if preferred, a suitable object can be placed in different places while the class directs its next move:

'Take it away. Now put it back. Now take it out . . .'

If you don't want me to stay here, I'll *go away*.

You're standing in my way and I can't *get past*.

The fence was much too high for them to *climb over*.

When you've finished with my books, please *bring* them *back*.

I felt so dizzy that the whole room seemed to be *going round*.

His finger was stuck in the bottle and he couldn't *get it out*.

It's a very annoying dog because it keeps *jumping up*.

Please *take* your muddy boots *off* before you come inside.

Some idiomatic prepositional verbs

IN PAIRS

Prepositional verbs (verbs + prepositions) have previously been practised in units 27 and 28. Perhaps refer back to these.

This exercise practises some common idiomatic (non-literal) prepositional verbs.

I don't feel *like* going out for lunch today.

He's working *on* a new book about the supernatural.

She's looking *for* someone to look *after* her children.

If you ever need a babysitter, just send *for* me.

They spent a week in the capital and then made *for* the country.

Driving when you're drunk is asking *for* trouble.

Young Billy takes *after* old Bill, his father.

Those yellow shoes don't go *with* your green trousers.

Little Sally looks *like* her mother, doesn't she?

The letters FCE stand *for* First Certificate in English.

Please get out of the way, I can't see *through* you!

Can you call *for* me at 8 – I'll be ready.

I find it quite difficult to get used *to* foreign food.

Prepositions and particles

IN PAIRS

Two of the difficulties students have in using phrasal verbs and prepositional verbs are:

a) the position of the particle or preposition in a sentence, and

b) the stress pattern of such sentences:

    She rán down the hǐll. (preposition)

    She wrŏte dŏwn the addrĕss. (particle)

Devote some time with the class to the presentation of the exercise, making sure everyone sees the difference between a particle and a preposition. Then get the pairs to cross out the incorrect sentences.

When they have done this, make sure they can read the correct sentences aloud with the right stress patterns.

He jumped off the cliff.	~~He jumped the cliff off.~~
~~They opened up them.~~	They opened up their presents.
~~He looked the children after.~~	He looked after them.
I'll play the recording back.	~~I'll play back it.~~
It's hard work bringing up children.	~~It's hard work bringing up them.~~
The car drove over the bridge.	~~The car drove the bridge over.~~
He walked past it.	~~He walked the shop past.~~

Rewrite the sentences

IN PAIRS   (or as homework)

This exercise shows that formal-style 'normal' verbs often have phrasal or prepositional verb synonyms in colloquial style. Perhaps begin by getting students to identify which of the verbs in the list are phrasal verbs and which are prepositional verbs:

> *take off*, for example, here is a prepositional verb (though there is also a phrasal verb *take off*, used to describe aircraft – see unit 39).

I asked if he wanted to take off his coat.
Let's lift up our glasses and drink to the happy couple.
I spent a happy hour looking at them working.
I'll always look on you as one of my best friends.
Someone has taken away my coat from the hall.
Press this button and these little wheels will spin round.
If necessary you should ask for further information.
The firemen managed to put out the fire.
Do please call on me if you're in the area.
I came across these old school photos in the attic.
I don't like the way he keeps on staring at me.
If you know her number you can ring her up.
If you could hold on a moment I'll see if she's available.
A good friend will always stand by you.
Now you've finished you can sit back.

▶→ Extra activity

IN PAIRS

Ask the pairs to compose a paragraph using six of the verbs from this unit. The topic should be one that is in the news or which has been discussed in class recently.

39 PHRASAL AND PREPOSITIONAL VERBS II

Summary

Practice in using some common idiomatic intransitive phrasal verbs:
come out, take off, stop off, stop over, set off, set out, get on, check in, check out, get together, wear out, go off, join in, go on, carry on, keep on, break down.
e.g. *Roses come out in the summer.*
The plane took off on time.

Using some common idiomatic transitive phrasal verbs:
take something away, turn something on, turn something down, turn something off, leave something on, make something up, etc.
e.g. *Please take this soup away.*
He turned on the radio.
I asked him to turn it down.

Using some common phrasal verbs consisting of *to be* + particle:
be over, be up, be on, be out, be off, be along, be in
e.g. *The war was over.*
I was up till midnight.
Your time is up.

(*Practical English Usage* 492)

Relevant errors

☆ The plane took on time off.
☆ We decided to call off it.
☆ Your time is along now.
☆ I don't like that music, please turn off.

Some idiomatic phrasal verbs

IN PAIRS

Students doing these exercises may be dismayed that there are thousands of idiomatic phrasal verbs in English and indeed many different meanings for many of them:

go off¹ *v adv* **1** [I0] **a** to explode **b** to ring or sound loudly: *The* ALARM *went off when the thieves got in* **2** [I0] (of food) to go bad: *This milk has gone off* **3** [I0] *infml* to lose skill, quality, etc.: *These classes have gone off since we had a new teacher.*|*The book goes off after the first 50 pages* **4** [I0] to cease to be felt: *The pain went off after 3 treatments* **5** [L9] to succeed or fail; COME OFF (3): *"How did your plan go off?" "It went off very well, thank you"* **6** [I0] to fall asleep or lose consciousness: *Has the baby gone off yet?* —compare GET OFF (4), DROP OFF (3) **7** [I0] to cease operation: *The heating goes off at night.*|*The lights went off* **8 go off with** *not fml* to take away without permission: *She's gone off with my book!*|*The milkman's gone off with my wife!*
go off² *v prep* [T1] to lose interest in or liking for: *I've gone off coffee, give me some tea*

go on¹ *v adv* **1** [I0] to take place or happen: *There's a wedding going on at the church.*|*What's going on here?* **2** [I0] GET ALONG (2) **3** [I0 (*at*)] to keep complaining or scolding: *She's always going on at her husband* **4** [I0] also **run on** *not fml*— to keep talking: *She does go on so!* **5** [I0 (*with*),3,4] to continue without stopping, or after a stop: *Go on, I'm listening.*|*Go on with your work* **6** [L9] to behave continually in a certain way: *If he goes on like this he'll lose his job.*|*To judge by the way he's going on, he's very nervous about something* **7** [I0] (of time) to pass: *As time went on, things began to change.*|*As the day went on, it became hotter* **8** [L9 (*for*)] *infml esp. BrE* to support oneself (at the stated level); MANAGE (3): *How did you go on for money while you were out of work?* **9** to be put into operation: *The heating goes on later.*|*The lights went on* **10 go on** (**with you**)! I don't believe you! **11 to be going/go on with** *infml esp. BrE* (to use) for the moment: *Here's £3 to be going on with. I'll give you some more tomorrow*
go on² *v prep* [T1 *no pass.*] to use as a reason, proof, or base for further action: *We were just going on what you yourself had said.*|*A bloody handkerchief and the name "Margaret" were all the police had to go on to catch the killer*

(extract from *Longman Dictionary of Contemporary English*)

However, reassure them that:

a) If they do try to learn and use many of the more colloquial ones, it may sound strange or even ridiculous to a native speaker;

b) Understanding a wide range of phrasal verbs *is* important, but not using them all;

c) The phrasal verbs practised in this unit are the important ones they do need to be able to use;
d) There are often synonymous 'normal' verbs that can be used instead of phrasal verbs: *deteriorate* for *go off*, *continue* for *go on*, etc.

We set off/out early in the morning.
We intended to stop off/over in Paris.
There was a thunderstorm but the plane flew on.
But soon the pilot decided to turn back to London.

As soon as I arrived at the hotel I checked in.
The lift was worn out.
Most days it broke down after breakfast.
I met some nice people and we got on well.
We arranged to get together after our holiday.
At the end of my stay I checked out.

Whenever there are party games I like to join in.
During the party all the lights went off.
We kept on playing games in the dark.
Suddenly there was a bang like a bomb going off.
Then the lights all went on again.

More idiomatic phrasal verbs

IN PAIRS

This long exercise can be done in two separate parts:
a) finding the right phrasal verbs
b) writing the correct grammatical forms of them in the spaces.

When this has been done, you can help students to remember the phrasal verbs by running through the exercise again like this:
Teacher: This music's too loud, can you please . . .
Class: Turn it down.
and so on.

Let's hear some music on the radio. Can you *turn it on?*
That's much too loud. Please *turn it down.*
Oh, the news is on, could you *turn it up* now please?
Oh dear, the news is so depressing, I'd like you to *turn it off.*
But if you want to hear it, please do *leave it on.*

I've got this very complicated form and I've got to *fill it in*.
I've put the wrong date so I'd better *cross it out*.
I can't *work out* why they want to know all this.
I don't know my grandmother's maiden name so I'll just *make it up*.
I've had enough of this: could you please *take it away*.

I wanted to *call off* my meeting with Mr Brown.
So I *rang up* first thing in the morning.
I had to wait while the operator tried to *put me through*.
His secretary said he was busy and asked me to *ring back*.
I told her that I wanted him to *call me back* immediately.
And then I threatened to *call off* the whole deal.

He's had a nervous breakdown and nobody knows what *brought it on*.
Bringing up four children is an awful strain.
And last year he had to *give up* his evening job.
Now someone else will have to *carry out* all his duties.
He says he's going to *give away* all his money.

Chess is a great game – why don't you *take it up?*
When Mr Brown arrives please *show him in*.
He looked the wrong way before crossing and I nearly *ran him over*.
Take a piece of paper and *cut it up* into four equal-size pieces.
If you don't understand this word you'd better *look it up*.
It'll help you remember these words if you *write them down*.

Be + particle

IN PAIRS

Point out that the phrases listed can all be used instead of the phrasal verbs if
students prefer them or find them easier to use.

Something has gone wrong, you look worried.
He is out of bed all night before an exam.
The lecture takes place at 7.30.
The party has finished and it's time to leave.
I won't be at home till 7, then I'll be at home all evening.
See you later, I'll arrive about 8.
Your time has finished, so stop writing now.   ⟫→

It is his responsibility to decide.
The match is cancelled because of rain.
His new book is being published in the spring.

▶→ Extra activity

IN PAIRS OR AS HOMEWORK

Get students to use six of the verbs from this unit in a single paragraph.

40 WORD ORDER

Summary

Practice in arranging modifiers (i.e. adjectives, nouns and adverbs that come before a noun) in the correct order:

NO.	SIZE, CONDITION, QUALITY, etc.	COLOUR	ORIGIN	MATERIAL	PURPOSE	NOUN
two	big soft	green	Greek	woollen	fisherman's	jerseys
one	small old	blue	Venetian	glass	flower	vase
etc.						

Placing adverbs correctly in pre-, mid- and post- position in a sentence:

PRE-

Suddenly I had toothache.
Yesterday I had toothache.
Recently I had toothache.
†*In bed I had toothache.*
†*Certainly I had toothache.*
**Never I have toothache.*
**Really badly I had toothache.*

MID-

I suddenly had toothache.
**I yesterday had toothache.*
I recently had toothache.
**I had in bed toothache.*
I certainly had toothache.
I never have toothache.
**I really badly had toothache.*

POST-

I had toothache suddenly.
I had toothache yesterday.
I had toothache recently.
I had toothache in bed.
**I had toothache certainly.*
†*I have toothache never.*
I had toothache really badly.

*Not normally acceptable
†Theoretically correct, but not a 'comfortable' position

Using adverbs that are normally placed in mid-position in a sentence:
never, always, often, usually, once, rarely, hardly ever, frequently, ever, obviously, clearly, surely, probably, presumably, certainly, apparently, almost, nearly, completely, just, hardly, really   ⟫→

e.g. *I have never eaten chocolates.*
  I never eat chocolates.
  I can never eat chocolates.
  I never have chocolates.
  These chocolates will never be eaten.

(*Practical English Usage* 15, 16, 17, 19, 23, 24, 25)

Relevant errors

☆ Five plastic transparent French umbrellas.
☆ Never I have headaches.
☆ She in bed eats chocolates.
☆ She fell nearly over.

Modifiers

IN PAIRS

These enormously long phrases are unlikely to crop up in real life, of course, but the rules they illustrate still hold good for shorter phrases:
  one American science book
  two large blue hats
  etc.

Five large transparent plastic raincoats.
Six large bright green tropical house plants.
Seven beautiful white Japanese ceramic flower vases.
Eight fascinating old German guide books.
Nine modern Italian metal door handles.
Ten wobbly Swedish plastic bicycles.

Get each pair to produce two more similar phrases beginning:
  '*eleven . . .* ' and '*twelve . . .* '

Adverbs

IN PAIRS

First, with the whole class, look at the examples and discuss the concept of 'comfortable' positioning of adverbs. Show that, for example:

> *In bed I had toothache*

and *I had in bed toothache*

both 'feel' wrong or uncomfortable. The actual rules of use are quite complex but by this time most students will have acquired a feeling for accuracy and comfortableness. This exercise exploits this feeling.

I'm ⋀ going to Italy for my holidays.	probably
She was waiting for me ⋀ .	indoors
⋀ He's leaving the country ⋀ .	tomorrow
She sings and dances ⋀ .	beautifully
I stayed in the library and worked ⋀ .	hard
⋀ The door ⋀ opened ⋀ and a hand appeared.	slowly
He plays the piano ⋀ .	very well
You'll have to work ⋀ to finish on time.	fast
They write to their parents ⋀ .	weekly
They hid the presents ⋀ .	behind the sofa

Mid-position adverbs

IN PAIRS

First, with the whole class, look at the examples and point out the implications of the idea of mid-position when there is an auxiliary verb in the sentence. (The traditional concept of 'frequency adverbs' is an unhelpful one since it seems to include *twice* and *three times*, while excluding *almost*, *nearly*, etc. It makes better sense to exploit students' acquired knowledge and feelings for accuracy, than to attempt to categorise adverbs arbitrarily.)

I've ⋀ enjoyed Westerns.	always
I've ⋀ finished my work.	just
You'll ⋀ be met at the airport.	certainly
⋀ He ⋀ shouldn't have done that ⋀ .	surely
Oops! I ⋀ fell over.	nearly
He's ⋀ going to be late.	probably
I can ⋀ understand him.	hardly
She ⋀ loses her temper.	rarely
It's ⋀ very difficult.	obviously
Things won't ⋀ improve.	ever

Point out any other positions that might be 'comfortable'.

167

Rearrange the words

IN PAIRS

This is a problem-solving activity as a final enjoyable round-up on word-order in sentences. Some of the proverbs may need to be explained afterwards:

The pen is mightier than the sword.
If at first you don't succeed try, try and try again.
It takes all sorts to make a world.
If a thing is worth doing it's worth doing well.
Rome wasn't built in a day.
When in Rome do as the Romans do.
It's no use crying over spilt milk.
Every cloud has a silver lining.
All good things must come to an end.

▸→ Extra activity

IN PAIRS

When the pairs have finished the exercise above, get them to compose three or four more sentences. Then they should rewrite them with the words jumbled up (as in the previous exercise) and give the jumbled sentences to another pair to rearrange. For example:

I you this enjoyed hope in and students the your book have doing activities!

Key to communication activities in Student's Book

Details of each activity are given in the relevant teaching notes for each unit in this book.

Unit No.	Activity title	Communication activities		
1	It's not very clear	A: 1	B: 6	
2	Your favourite colour's red, isn't it?	A: 3	B: 9	C: 12
3	Have you ever ... ?	A: 5	B: 15	
	Famous men	A: 18	B: 26	
5	What's going on?	A: 22	B: 32	
6	What's in a name?	A: 17	B: 21	
	Did you say 'court' or 'caught'?	key in activity 46		
	A E I O U	A: 4	B: 20	
	Eh? Oh! Ow!!	A: 10	B: 24	
8	What does it look like?	A: 14	B: 27	
9	Go straight on until ...	A: 11	B: 57	
10	I'd like you to ...	A: 8	B: 19	
	Enjoy your flight!	key in activity 7		
11	Shopping lists	A: 2	B: 13	
15	Stop!	A: 33	B: 39	
	Don't forget!	A: 38	B: 47	
17	Why do you think ... ?	A: 36	B: 41	
19	Guess what!	A: 34	B: 51	
20	In other words	A: 31	B: 48	
26	What's she called?	A: 35	B: 44	
	What's it about?	A: 37	B: 43	C: 56
29	Being ...	A: 29	B: 49	
32	Adjectives → nouns	keys in activities 40 and 55		
	Verbs → nouns	keys in activities 52 and 30		
33	What's the opposite of ... ?	key in activity 42		
34	How much? How many?	A: 28	B: 53	
	Arithmetic	A: 16	B: 45	
36	Uncles	A: 23	B: 54	
37	The reasons why ...	A: 25	B: 50	